Classic Sermons

Classic Sermons

Kenneth E. Hagin

FAITH LIBRARY PUBLICATIONS

Unless otherwise indicated, all Scripture quotations in this volume are from the *King James Version* of the Bible.

Second Printing 1993

ISBN 0-89276-516-X

In the U.S. write:
Kenneth Hagin Ministries
P.O. Box 50126
Tulsa, OK 74150-0126

In Canada write:
Kenneth Hagin Ministries
P.O. Box 335
Islington (Toronto), Ontario
Canada, M9A 4X3

BOOKS BY KENNETH E. HAGIN

Following God's Plan For Your Life
The Triumphant Church
The Price Is Not Greater Than God's Grace (Mrs. Oretha Hagin)

MINIBOOKS (A partial listing)

* *The New Birth*
* *Why Tongues?*
* *In Him*
* *God's Medicine*
* *You Can Have What You Say*
  How To Write Your Own Ticket With God
* *Don't Blame God*
* *Words*
  Plead Your Case
* *How To Keep Your Healing*
  The Bible Way To Receive the Holy Spirit
  I Went to Hell
  How To Walk in Love
  The Precious Blood of Jesus
* *Love Never Fails*
  Learning To Flow With the Spirit of God
  The Glory of God
  Hear and Be Healed
  Knowing What Belongs to Us
  Your Faith in God Will Work

BOOKS BY KENNETH HAGIN JR.

* *Man's Impossibility — God's Possibility*
  Because of Jesus
  How To Make the Dream God Gave You Come True
  The Life of Obedience
  God's Irresistible Word
  Healing: Forever Settled
  Don't Quit! Your Faith Will See You Through
  The Untapped Power in Praise
  Listen to Your Heart
  What Comes After Faith?

MINIBOOKS (A partial listing)

* *Faith Worketh by Love*
  Blueprint for Building Strong Faith
* *Seven Hindrances to Healing*
* *The Past Tense of God's Word*
  Faith Takes Back What the Devil's Stolen
  "The Prison Door Is Open — What Are You Still Doing Inside?"
  How To Be a Success in Life
  Get Acquainted With God
  Showdown With the Devil
  Unforgiveness
  Ministering to the Brokenhearted

*These titles are also available in Spanish. Information about other foreign translations of several of the above titles (i.e., Finnish, French, German, Indonesian, Polish, Russian, etc.) may be obtained by writing to: Kenneth Hagin Ministries, P.O. Box 50126, Tulsa, Oklahoma 74150-0126.

Contents

Preface

Preface

In the mid-1940s during a time of prayer, God spoke to my heart about my future ministry.

The Lord told me that by the time I reached sixty-five years of age, two of the main outreaches of my ministry would be radio and the printed page. The Lord said to me, "The best means to spread the gospel is through the printed page."

That word from the Lord to me has certainly come to pass. Today more than forty-seven million Faith Library books are in print, with seventy-two of those titles translated into twenty-six foreign languages.

But perhaps the most well-known outreach of Kenneth Hagin Ministries through the printed page is *The Word of Faith* magazine, which was started in 1968. Although over the years the design of the magazine has changed several times, its message of truth and faith in God's Word has remained the same.

The messages in this book reflect some of the major themes I have preached over my years of ministry. These sermons were taken from articles printed throughout twenty-five years of *The Word of Faith*. As you read them, let the truth of God's Word become established in your heart and transform defeat into victory in your life!

Chapter 1

Get Acquainted With Your Heavenly Father

For this cause I bow my knees unto the
FATHER of our Lord Jesus Christ,
Of whom the whole FAMILY IN HEAVEN
AND EARTH is named.
> — Ephesians 3:14,15

Spiritually speaking, there are only two families on the earth: the family of God and the family of Satan. Every person, regardless of heritage or background, belongs to one of those two families. Which family do *you* belong to? Who is your father — God or Satan?

The only way you can be *delivered out of* the family of Satan is to be *born into* the family of God (John 3:3; Col. 1:13). You must receive Jesus as your Savior and be born again in order to belong to the family of God and call God your Heavenly Father.

Once you are born again, you begin to grow spiritually as you get to know your Heavenly Father. The number one way you become better acquainted with God the Father is *through His Word.* Smith Wigglesworth once said, "I can't understand God by *feelings.* I understand God by what the *Word* says about Him. He is everything the Word says He is."

You see, many people want to get acquainted with

1

the Father through experiences. And it's true, you can learn some things about God the Father through different experiences in life. But the number one way to get to know the Father is through His Word. In the Word we find out about the Father's nature and how much He loves and cares for us.

What does the Word say about our Heavenly Father? In the Gospels, Jesus always presented God as a loving Father.

JOHN 3:16
16 For GOD SO LOVED the world, that he gave his only begotten Son, that whosoever believeth in him should not perish, but have everlasting life.

JOHN 16:27
27 For THE FATHER himself LOVETH YOU, because ye have loved me, and have believed that I came out from God.

It was difficult for the Jews to understand what Jesus was saying when He talked about a Father of love. They had only known God as a God of law and justice — and that *is* one side of God.

But Jesus was presenting the Fatherhood side of God. He was presenting the very nature of the Father, for the Bible says God is love (1 John 4:16). Jesus revealed God as a loving Father who cares for our every need.

MATTHEW 6:8,26
8 Be not ye therefore like unto them [the Gentiles]: **for YOUR FATHER knoweth what things ye have need of, before ye ask him. . . .**

26 Behold the fowls of the air: for they sow not, neither do they reap, nor gather into barns; yet YOUR HEAVENLY FATHER feedeth them. Are ye not much better than they?

Notice the utter tenderness in this picture of the Father caring for His children. Our Heavenly Father knows our needs, and He desires to meet them before we even ask Him for help!

Because God is my Father, I like to do what Paul is talking about in Ephesians 3:14,15: *"For this cause I bow my knees unto the Father of our Lord Jesus Christ"* (v. 14). I like to get down on my knees and say, "I bow my knees unto the Father of our Lord Jesus Christ of whom the whole family in Heaven and earth is named." That word "family" takes God out of a harsh religious context and makes our relationship to the Father so real and intimate.

We're a part of the Father's family. That fact has nothing in the world to do with religion. Religion is harsh and cold, but Christianity is a relationship with a God who is a loving Father.

Many Christians have a difficult time comprehending God as a Father who loves and cares for them. Often Christians have been religiously taught to fear and to shrink from a God of justice. They have the idea that God is like a judge who sits up in Heaven and looks for a chance to punish people the moment they make a mistake.

But, no, God is love! Thank God for the Father's love which Jesus came to reveal to us.

In Matthew 6, Jesus says more about the Father's

care for His children.

> **MATTHEW 6:31-33**
> **31 Therefore take no thought, saying, What shall we eat? or, What shall we drink? or, Wherewithal shall we be clothed?**
> **32 (For after all these things do the Gentiles seek:) for YOUR HEAVENLY FATHER knoweth that ye have need of all these things.**
> **33 But seek ye first the kingdom of God, and his righteousness; and all these things SHALL BE ADDED UNTO YOU.**

Some people have been religiously taught to read that last verse: "All these things shall be *taken away from* you." They think if they put God first, they won't ever have anything.

But that's not what Jesus said. He said the things you need will be *added* to you as you seek first the Kingdom of God. That promise proves your Father's love and care for you.

Look at Matthew 6:34. Jesus said, *"Take therefore no thought for the morrow. . . ."* Another translation says, "Be not anxious for tomorrow." This verse shows us that the Father doesn't want His children full of worry and anxiety because He loves us and wants to meet our every need.

So have no worry or anxiety. Do not fret. You can be sure of this one fact: *As you trust God with your life, He will take a Father's place and perform a Father's part in your life.* He is your Father, and He loves you and cares for you with an everlasting love (Jer. 31:3).

In the Book of John, Jesus shows the Father's desire for intimate fellowship with His children.

JOHN 14:21,23
21 He that hath my commandments, and keepeth them, he it is that loveth me: and he that loveth me SHALL BE LOVED OF MY FATHER, and I will love him, and will manifest myself to him. . . .
23 . . . If a man love me, he will keep my words: and my Father will love him, and we will come unto him, and MAKE OUR ABODE WITH HIM.

That phrase, "make our abode" means the Father and Jesus will come and take up permanent residence in you as you obey God's Word. Here is a revelation of the Heavenly Father's desire to have continual fellowship with you, His child.

Notice Jesus emphasized two points in John 14:21,23. First, He talked about *our* responsibility when He said we are to keep His commandments. Jesus summed up all His commandments in one when He said, *"A new commandment I give unto you, That YE LOVE ONE ANOTHER; as I have loved you . . ."* (John 13:34).

We don't need to be so concerned about obeying all the commandments of the Old Testament because the Bible says *love* is the fulfilling of the law (Rom. 13:10). In other words, if you keep that one commandment and continually walk in love toward others, you will automatically fulfill every other commandment!

The second point Jesus emphasized was the Father's love: *". . . he that loveth me SHALL BE LOVED OF MY FATHER . . ."* (John 14:21). The great

Father God is a God of love, and His very love nature compels Him to care for and provide for His children.

Think about natural parents. Most parents want the best for their children and know how to give their children good things. Well, the Bible asks the question, "If natural parents know how to give good things to *their* children, *how much more* does our Heavenly Father know how to give good gifts to *His* children!"

> **MATTHEW 7:11**
> 11 If ye then, being evil [or natural], **know how to give good gifts unto your children, HOW MUCH MORE shall your Father which is in heaven give good things to them that ask him?**

What are the *good things* the Father wants to give to His children? If you have a need, it is a good thing to have your need met. For instance, if you were hurting, it would be a *good thing* to be healed. The Bible says that healing is good: ". . . [Jesus] *went about DOING GOOD, and HEALING all that were oppressed of the devil* . . ." (Acts 10:38). Healing is a good thing, and your Heavenly Father delights to give you the good gift of healing, as well as anything else you might need.

If that's difficult for you to accept, here is an important fact from the Word of God you need to know: *We can enjoy the same relationship with the Father God that Jesus did when Jesus walked on the earth.* Let me prove that statement to you from Jesus' prayer to the Father in the Book of John.

> **JOHN 17:23**
> 23 I in them [believers], **and thou in me, that they**

may be made perfect in one; and that the world may know that THOU hast sent me, and HAST LOVED THEM, AS THOU HAST LOVED ME.

Get ahold of this fact: *God the Father doesn't love Jesus any more than He loves you.* Walking in the light of that one truth will make all the difference in the world in how you live your life.

For instance, since the Father loves you as much as He loves Jesus, then you never have to be afraid of life's problems.

Romans 8:31 says, ". . . *If God be for us, who can be against us?*" What can man do to a child of God whom the Father loves and protects? The Father was for His Son, Jesus, as He walked upon the earth, and He is for *you* too.

Let's look at an important statement Jesus made about His relationship with His Father.

JOHN 16:32
32 Behold, the hour cometh, yea, is now come, that ye shall be scattered, every man to his own, and shall leave me alone: and yet I AM NOT ALONE, BECAUSE THE FATHER IS WITH ME.

Jesus was telling His disciples, "You are all going to leave Me and be scattered. But even so, I am not alone. My Father is always with Me." And if Jesus could say that, so can we, because the Father loves us just as He loved Jesus.

In the face of any test or trial, you can say, "I'm not alone because the Father is with me. If everyone forsakes me, I'm still not alone, because my Father will never forsake me!"

Some people start feeling sorry for themselves if a few friends forsake them. They have a pity party and think, *No one loves me.* But that's just not true. People who think this way need to get acquainted with the Father through the Word. Their Heavenly Father loves them, and He promised never to leave or forsake them (Deut. 31:6,8; Heb. 13:5)!

When you get acquainted with the Father through His Word and begin to walk in the light of what you learn about Him, you won't need to have pity parties anymore. Your "blue days" will be over because you'll *know* that you are not alone. The Father is always with you just as He was always with Jesus. Therefore, you can always feel safe and secure in His love.

My natural father left my mother and us kids when I was only six years old. But I can remember one incident with him which illustrates that feeling of safety a child has in knowing his daddy is near. One day when I was only a little fellow, my father and I walked uptown together. While we were walking in the midst of a crowd of people, we somehow became separated.

I remember how scared I was. I frantically looked around for my daddy. When I finally saw him, I ran as hard as I could to him and grabbed ahold of his finger. Once I had a tight hold on his finger, everything was fine again; I wasn't afraid anymore. I knew no harm would come to me, because my daddy was there with me.

How much more should that be true with your Heavenly Father? Because your Heavenly Father promised never to leave or forsake you, *you are not alone.* If you're feeling afraid or overwhelmed by life's tests and trials, just get ahold of the finger of God and walk on!

We've looked at several statements Jesus made relative to the Father. Against the backdrop of these powerful statements about the Father's love, other scriptures take on new light and become more real to us.

For instance, let's look at a familiar scripture in *The Amplified Bible.*

1 PETER 5:7 *(Amplified)*
7 Casting the whole of your care — all your anxieties, all your worries, all your concerns, once and for all — on Him; for He CARES FOR YOU affectionately, and CARES ABOUT YOU watchfully.

You should read that scripture as if your Heavenly Father is speaking directly to you, because this *is* a message from the very heart of God to you. He wants you to put an end to worry, doubt, and fear in your life.

How do you get rid of worry, doubt, and fear? By doing what this scripture says. Cast *all* of your care upon the Father. Abandon yourself to His love and care. Having done that, make sure you *leave* your burden with the Lord. When you have given your cares to the Father *once and for all*, don't pick them up again.

God tells us something similar in the Book of Philippians: "Do not fret or have any anxiety about *anything* . . ." (Phil. 4:6 *Amp.*). God is not an unjust Father. He loves us and wouldn't ask us to do something we couldn't do.

But what are we going to do if we can't worry? The rest of the verse tells us: ". . . in every circumstance and in everything *by prayer and petition* [definite requests] *with thanksgiving* continue to make your wants known to God."

Think what a difference it would make in people's lives if they would walk in the light of these scriptures! Some people go many places trying every way except *God's* way to receive deliverance and victory. They may receive temporary help, but they won't experience permanent victory until they practice being doers of the Word.

You will only experience victory by refusing to worry and fret about your problems and cares. Instead, take those cares to the Lord in prayer and thank Him for the answer. Your Father loves you. He is interested in you. If you will make your requests known to Him and wait in His Presence, He will help you understand what to do and give you the answers to your problems.

How much your Heavenly Father loves you! Wouldn't you like to know Him better? Take advantage of the access your Father has provided for you through Jesus (Eph. 2:18) and get acquainted with Him through His Word. Commune with Him in prayer, and be sure to cast all your cares upon Him.

As you come to know and experience for yourself the depth of the Father's love for you, doubts and fears that have plagued you in the past will be dispelled. As the Father loved Jesus, so He loves you. And because of the Father's great love for you, you are *never* alone!

Chapter 2
Godliness Is Profitable

But refuse profane and old wives' fables, and exercise thyself rather unto godliness.

For bodily exercise profiteth little: but GODLINESS IS PROFITABLE UNTO ALL THINGS, having promise of the life that now is, and of that which is to come. . . .

Meditate upon these things; give thyself wholly to them; THAT THY PROFITING MAY APPEAR TO ALL.

— 1 Timothy 4:7,8,15

Paul plainly said, ". . . *godliness is profitable* . . ." (v. 8). If anything is profitable, it pays off.

Thank God, there is profit in serving God. Living for God is not detrimental to a successful life. It is ". . . *profitable unto ALL things* . . ." (v. 8).

I think the Spirit of God knew there would be those who would say, "Well, yes, serving God will pay off in the *next* life. We may not have much to show for it in *this* life. In this life we wander like a beggar through the heat and the cold. But when it's all over and we get to the *other* side, it will be different. There's a great day *coming* when we've left *this* vale of tears and sorrow."

Well, thank God, there *is* a great day coming. But Paul said, ". . . *godliness is profitable unto all things, having promise of THE LIFE THAT NOW IS* . . ."!

"Having promise" — that's present tense. The life that now is means right now *in this present world*.

There is a life that *now is*, and there is a life that *is to come*. I'm more concerned about the life that now is than I am about the life that is to come. Because the life that "now is" is the life I'm living right now.

If you listen to some people, you get the impression that God only promises us success and victory in the *next* life. Their basic attitude about the Christian walk boils down to this: "You can get saved in this life, all right, but after you're saved, that's about it. You've had it! You're left to the mercy of the devil. You're left to the mercy of the world. You can't expect much in this life."

But that's not what Paul said to Timothy, who was a young minister. Paul said, "Yes, godliness has a promise of the life that is to come. But godliness is also profitable unto *all things*." Godliness is not just profitable to the spirit, but it is also profitable to the soul, the body, and in the material realm. Why? Because godliness is profitable unto *all* things, even in this present life!

There are at least four things that godliness ensures or guarantees.

First, godliness ensures *protection*.

If you have property or anything of value, you protect it. Once I was at my son's house, and I saw his dog, King, chewing on a shoe. I said, "Hey, King has one of your shoes!"

"Oh, he's not hurting anything," Ken said. "That's

an old shoe we threw away." Ken didn't care about protecting that shoe because it didn't amount to anything; it had no value to him.

But we're not like that old shoe. We belong to God! We amount to something! We are so valuable to Him, He gave His Son to die for us to redeem us. We are precious to God, and He protects us!

I like the account of the woman with the issue of blood because for one thing, it shows that we are *somebody* to God. When the woman touched Jesus, He said, "Daughter, thy faith hath made thee whole" (Luke 8:48). Mark's account goes into more detail, and I usually preach from it. But there is something I especially like about Luke's account along this line.

As Luke records the story, when Jesus stopped the procession going toward Jairus' house, He said, "*Somebody* touched me" (Luke 8:46). Jesus didn't say, "Nobody touched me." He said, "*Somebody* touched me!" Until that woman touched Jesus, she was a *nobody*. But when she touched Jesus, she became a *somebody*!

Let me explain what I mean by that. According to the Book of Leviticus, this poor woman with the issue of blood was in the same category as a leper. She was unclean. A leper had to segregate himself from other people. If somebody got close to him, he had to cry out, "Unclean! Unclean! I'm unclean!" A leper was a *nobody*.

But, bless God, Jesus said, "*Somebody* touched me." He transformed that woman from a *nobody* to a *somebody*. I want you to know, *you* are a *somebody* too.

You are somebody because you are a child of God.

You are a joint-heir with Jesus Christ — an equal heir. You are in the family of God. That's a *somebody!*

We are the Body of Christ, and we are precious in the sight of God. The Bible tells us that.

Writing to the Ephesians, Paul uses husbands and wives as an illustration of Christ and the Church. We can see in this passage how valuable we are to God.

> **EPHESIANS 5:25,28-30**
> **25 Husbands, love your wives, EVEN AS CHRIST ALSO LOVED THE CHURCH, and gave himself for it....**
> **28 So ought men to love their wives as their own bodies. He that loveth his wife loveth himself.**
> **29 For no man ever yet hated his own flesh; but NOURISHETH and CHERISHETH it, EVEN AS THE LORD THE CHURCH:**
> **30 For we are members of his body, of his flesh, and of his bones.**

Paul makes the statement, "No man has ever yet hated his own body" (v. 29), in regard to the beautiful marriage relationship between a husband and wife. But there's a further thought here, my friends, that I want to get over to you. We are the Body of Christ. We are *His* body.

A man's wife is bone of his bone and flesh of his flesh. And as Paul points out, we are bone of Christ's bone and flesh of His flesh!

Paul said that men were to nourish and cherish their wives. Then he said, *"This is a great mystery: but I speak concerning Christ and the church"* (Eph. 5:32).

In other words, we are precious to Jesus, and He nourishes and cherishes us.

If you have valuable property, you're going to protect it. You're not going to leave it out for the dogs to chew on. As a member of Christ's Body, you are precious and valuable to Jesus. And He has promised to protect you as you serve Him in this life.

Godliness guarantees protection, for godliness is profitable unto *all* things. Read Psalm 91 and learn about the protection that is yours because of your covenant with God.

Second, godliness ensures *promotion*.

Consider what God did for Joseph because Joseph stayed true to God. Yes, he was sold into captivity (Gen. 37:23-28). Yes, he was put into prison (Gen. 39:20). But God blessed him even in Egypt.

Ordinarily, a man would become bitter after spending years in prison. But because Joseph was faithful to God, God promoted him and made him prime minister of the greatest nation of that day (Gen. 41:38-41).

Did it pay to be faithful to God? Did godliness pay off? Did it pay to say "No!" to his master's wife when she tried to seduce him (Gen. 39:7-9)? A thousand times, yes!

Joseph spent many years in prison. Most men would have given up on God by then. But remember this: God doesn't settle up His accounts every Saturday night. God doesn't pay off the first of every month, or even the first of every year. But I want you to know, brother and sister, that someday payday in God is coming!

Preachers often use Galatians 6:7 as an evangelistic sermon: "... *whatsoever a man soweth, that shall he also reap.*" But Paul wasn't writing to sinners; he was writing to *Christians!* He wrote that epistle to be read throughout all the churches of Galatia.

Paul encouraged the Galatians not to faint, but to continue sowing into the Kingdom of God. He assured them that sooner or later they would reap the reward — the promotion — for their work in the Lord: "... *let us not be weary in well doing: for in due season we shall reap, if we faint not*" (Gal. 6:9).

The only way you can make it in ministry is to refuse to be weary in well doing. I've been in the ministry almost sixty years. Through the years I've had every reason in the world to be weary. But I've simply refused to be weary in well doing.

I preached faith when it didn't look like it was working for me. I preached faith boldly, bless God, without a dime in my pocket. I preached faith and prosperity boldly with bills stacked up all around me. I preached what the Word promises us in the face of insurmountable difficulties because I knew it was the *Word* of God!

If you think you're just going to float through life on flowery beds of ease, you've got another thought coming! God never promised you a life without trials. But He *has* promised you victory in the midst of the trials of life (John 16:33)!

As you are faithful to serve God, He *will* promote you. God always rewards faithfulness. But *you're* going to have to make the dedication and consecration to obey God. You will have to make that choice.

You're going to have to have the intestinal fortitude to say, "This is what God called me to do, and I'm going to do it, go over or under, sink or swim, live or die! I'm going to obey God!"

When we first got married, my wife and I made that kind of commitment. There was a time when it looked like all those things were going to happen too! It looked like we were going to sink. It looked like we were going to go under. It looked like we were going to die.

But I had meant it when I said, "I'm not going to turn back," because Jesus said, ". . . *No man, having put his hand to the plough, and looking back, is fit for the kingdom of God*" (Luke 9:62). I knew God wanted me to preach the gospel, even when it seemed nobody was listening.

I preached faith even when I was young in the ministry. People would say, "You know, that Brother Hagin is an odd character." And my friends would answer, "Yes, I don't understand him either."

You see, you're an oddity to others when you walk by faith and they're all walking by sight. You're an oddity to people when you refuse to worry. You're an oddity to people when in the midst of obeying God and preaching that God will promote you, you have to sell your automobile for junk and walk to your next meeting.

When that happened to me in my early days of field ministry, I told myself, *Praise God, I'm not going to stop, even if I do have to junk that old car. I'm still going. If I have to walk to get to my meetings, I'm still going. Sooner or later, God is going to promote me!* I might have been afoot, and the soles worn out of my shoes, but I *knew* God would promote me if I was faithful to what He had called me to do.

When I went through hard times like that, it wasn't that God was withholding His blessing from me. It was just the devil, trying to see if I really believed what I claimed I believed. You see, at every turn of the road, the devil will try to put up roadblocks in your path. He's going to try and put you to the test and see if you really believe God's Word.

The devil is the same accuser of the brethren he was in the Book of Job. The devil accused Job in the Presence of God (Job. 1:9-11). "Yeah, no wonder Job serves You," the devil said. "Just look. Everything is going smoothly for him. All his children are well. He's wealthy. Just take down the hedge and let me get to him. *Then* you'll see if he'll serve You!"

Satan is the god of this world (2 Cor. 4:4). You have to live in this world where Satan is god. The devil will accuse you and try to tempt you on every level. He'll try to throw up every obstacle he can to keep you from living the victorious life God has planned for you.

But if you'll believe the Word and do what it says, you won't be afraid even in the midst of a trial. I know that from experience.

I understand exactly how Peter could lie down and sleep soundly when they were planning to kill him the next day. Peter had no fear because he was trusting completely in God's power to deliver him. He was in faith! He was sleeping so soundly an angel had to smite him on the side to wake him up. Peter didn't even realize he was really awake until he was outside the prison (Acts 12:6-11).

In the same way, the Lord has enabled me to lie down and sleep soundly even in the midst of the most adverse circumstances. I could sleep even when nothing seemed to be going right. I was able to sleep in perfect peace because I *knew* that godliness is profitable. I knew if I would be faithful and not grow weary in well doing, in *due season* I would reap. I wanted to be ready to reap when the due season came!

Yes, many times it would have been easy to become weary. It would have been easy to quit. Absolutely. That would have been the easy way out. Just quit. Just give up.

My flesh wanted to quit. My mind wanted to quit. But something on the inside of me — the Word and the Holy Spirit — kept encouraging me to hold fast to my confession of faith.

Be a man or woman of the Word and of the Holy Spirit! In the midst of adversity, declare that the Word is true. Trials may come, but godliness *is* profitable. Just remain faithful to obey God even when the going gets hard, and sooner or later promotion day *will* come.

Third, godliness ensures *prosperity*.

When I talk about prosperity, I'm talking about

enjoying an *abundant supply* and *good success* in every area of life.

For example, the Bible says that as long as King Uzziah sought the Lord, God caused him to prosper (2 Chron. 26:5).

Furthermore, in the early days of Joshua's ministry, when he had to take the place of Moses as leader of the Israelites (think about having to take Moses' place!), God told Joshua exactly how to prosper and be successful.

> **JOSHUA 1:8**
> **8 This book of the law shall not depart out of thy mouth; but thou shalt MEDITATE therein day and night, that thou mayest OBSERVE TO DO according to all that is written therein: for THEN thou shalt make thy way PROSPEROUS, and then thou shalt have GOOD SUCCESS.**

Meditating on the Word and *acting* on the Word is the way to make your life prosperous. That's another way of saying that godliness is profitable unto all things.

Paul made a similar statement to Timothy in First Timothy 4:15: *"MEDITATE upon these things; give thyself wholly to them; that thy PROFITING may appear to all."* In other words, as you meditate on and practice the Word of God, everyone will be able to see you prosper in every area of your life.

Fourth, godliness ensures *perpetuity*.

The Bible teaches that godliness ensures perpetuity. That means God promises those who serve Him a long life on this earth and eternal life with Him.

In Psalm 91:14,16, God said, *"Because he hath set his love upon me. . . . With LONG LIFE will I satisfy him, and shew him my salvation."*

In Psalm 34:12,13, He said, *"What man is he that DESIRETH LIFE, and LOVETH MANY DAYS, that he may see good? Keep thy tongue from evil, and thy lips from speaking guile."*

In the New Testament, Peter quotes that same psalm: *"For he that will LOVE LIFE, and SEE GOOD DAYS, let him refrain his tongue from evil, and his lips that they speak no guile"* (1 Peter 3:10).

Notice there is always a connection between obedience, or godliness, and God's promise of a long life. We can see this again in God's promise to children who honor their parents.

EPHESIANS 6:1-3
1 Children, obey your parents in the Lord: for this is right.
2 Honour thy father and mother; which is the first commandment with promise;
3 That it may be WELL with thee, and THOU MAYEST LIVE LONG ON THE EARTH.

Teach your children while they're small to honor their parents so they can live long, full lives. When Ken and Pat were children, I read them this passage in Eph-

esians 6 nearly every day. That's the reason we never
had to take either one of them to the hospital. (Those
are not "well days" when you're in the hospital.)

Of course, someone always tries to argue, "I know
So-and-so, and he was a preacher, and one of his children died."

Well, that doesn't change the Bible. Maybe that
preacher was a good man and loved God with all of his
heart. But he may not have understood his covenant
rights in Christ for protection and perpetuity — long
life.

You see, the Bible says, *"The secret things belong
unto the Lord our God: but those things which are
revealed BELONG UNTO US and to OUR CHILDREN
for ever . . ."* (Deut. 29:29). When God's promise of perpetuity was revealed to me, I knew it belonged to my
children as well.

The Bible says we can believe God for long life here
on earth. But the Bible also says, ". . . *whosoever
believeth in him should not perish, but have EVER-
LASTING LIFE"* (John 3:16). Everlasting life is long
life, isn't it?

Just because I leave this body doesn't mean the real
me — my spirit man — is dead! Man's spirit never dies.
Jesus said, *". . . whosoever liveth and believeth in me
SHALL NEVER DIE . . ."* (John 11:26).

Of course, if Jesus tarries His coming, we will
depart from these bodies at physical death. But our
spirit man will live on, and so we will ever be with the
Lord (1 Thess. 4:17)! Everlasting life is perpetuity!

Your loved ones who died in the Lord are not really dead. Their body is dead, but *they* just moved out of their *earthly* house into *Father's* House (2 Cor. 5:1). Glory to God!

Did the Psalmist David say, "Surely goodness and mercy shall follow me all the days of my life: and I will dwell in the house of the Lord *until I die*"? No, no, no! He said, ". . . *I will dwell in the house of the Lord FOR EVER*" (Ps. 23:6). Forever! *Perpetuity*. That means forever and ever.

Godliness means to live for God. It's profitable. It pays off in this life. In *this* life! And in *the life to come*.

So be determined to live for God. You will find that as you do, your profiting will be apparent to all who observe your walk with God. You will be surrounded by God's *protection*; overtaken by God's *promotion*; supplied with God's *prosperity*; and sustained by God's *perpetuity*!

Chapter 3
Who's Who in Hell

Every human being on the earth will have to face eternity one day. When a person dies, he is not dead like a dog or like some kind of animal. No, when a person dies, he faces *eternity*: The righteous enter into "life eternal" (Matt. 25:46), and the unrighteous are cast into hell or the lake of fire (Rev. 20:15). The lake of fire is the final dwelling place for the unrighteous, for those whose names are not written in the Lamb's Book of Life (Rev. 20:15).

We should thank God for the revelation His Word gives us concerning Heaven because those of us who have accepted Jesus Christ as Savior and have been born again are going there one day. We're Heaven-bound if we're in Christ!

The revelation concerning Heaven is good news. But we should also thank God for the revelation His Word gives us concerning *hell*. Those who don't know Jesus are *not* Heaven-bound. And we as Christians need to reach these people with the gospel and let them know there is a Heaven to gain and a hell to shun, because when people who are unsaved die and leave this world, they go to hell.

The Bible gives us some detail about hell in the Gospel of Mark.

MARK 9:43,44
43 And if thy hand offend thee, cut it off: it is bet-

**ter for thee to enter into life maimed, than having
two hands to go INTO HELL, INTO THE FIRE
THAT NEVER SHALL BE QUENCHED.
44 Where their worm dieth not, and the fire is not
quenched.**

We see here that hell is a place of unquenchable
fire.

Notice that verse 43 says, ". . . *if thy hand offend
thee, cut it off. . . .*" We know, of course, this verse is not
talking about cutting off your natural hand. It simply
means there are some things in life that a person needs
to "cut off" or give up.

For instance, it would be better for a person to
accept Jesus Christ and give up his life of sin and go to
Heaven, than it would be for him to reject Jesus, hold
on to his sin, and go to hell, where the worm dies not
and the fire is not quenched.

We also know that hell is a place of everlasting punishment.

MATTHEW 25:46
**46 And these shall go away into EVERLASTING
PUNISHMENT: but the righteous into LIFE ETER-
NAL.**

In many places in the Bible we can read about what
hell is like. But the Bible also gives us some detail
about the *kinds of people* who go there.

PSALM 9:17
**17 The WICKED shall be turned INTO HELL, and
ALL THE NATIONS THAT FORGET GOD.**

Notice this verse says, *"The wicked shall be turned into hell. . . ."* Most people would agree that there ought to be an eternal dwelling place for those who are wicked and mean. And there is. I'm sorry to say that there have been many wicked and mean people who have lived on this earth, whose eternal dwelling place is hell. The Bible says the wicked or the unredeemed go to hell (Ps. 9:17). You see, unless a person is born again, whether he acts wickedly on this earth or not, he cannot see the Kingdom of God (John 3:3).

So we know from the Bible that the wicked go to hell. But the rest of Psalm 9:17 says, *". . . and ALL THE NATIONS THAT FORGET GOD."* You see, you don't have to be wicked to miss Heaven and go to hell. All you have to do is fail to accept Jesus Christ as Savior and forget Him! All you have to do is leave God out of your life.

Just leave God out and neglect to accept Jesus Christ as your Savior and Lord, and you'll go to hell just as quickly as the worse wretch that ever walked the streets of your city! On the other hand, by accepting Jesus Christ, even the worst sinner can be born again and miss hell and make Heaven his home.

There's a book which lists people in the English-speaking world who have achieved a certain degree of prominence in the arts and sciences, in business, and in the professions. Sometimes it's interesting to know "who's who" in this life. But the Bible also gives us a "who's who" in hell, so to speak. For instance, it lists some of the unredeemed who will spend eternity in hell.

REVELATION 21:8
8 But the FEARFUL, and UNBELIEVING, and
the ABOMINABLE, and MURDERERS, and
WHOREMONGERS, and SORCERERS, and IDOL-
ATERS, and all LIARS, shall have their part in the
lake which burneth with fire and brimstone:
which is the second death.

This scripture gives us a list of the kinds of unsaved
people who will go to hell. We know that those who
practice sin do not know the Lord (1 John 3:6-8), and
the Bible says without knowing Jesus Christ as Savior
and Lord, no man can see God (John 3:3; 14:6).

But a person need never go to hell if he will just do
what the Bible says and accept Jesus Christ as Savior
and Lord. The Bible says those who accept Jesus Christ
go to Heaven or into "life eternal," but those who do not
accept Jesus Christ will go into eternal torments and
punishment (Matt. 25:46; Luke 16:23).

So we can learn from the Bible about some of the
kinds of people who go to hell.

LUKE 16:19-23
19 There was a certain rich man, which was
clothed in purple and fine linen, and fared sump-
tuously every day:
20 And there was a certain beggar named
Lazarus, which was laid at his gate, full of sores,
21 And desiring to be fed with the crumbs which
fell from the rich man's table: moreover the dogs
came and licked his sores.
22 And it came to pass, that the beggar died, and
was carried by the angels into Abraham's bosom:
the rich man also died, and was buried;

> **23 And IN HELL he** [the rich man] **LIFT UP HIS
> EYES, BEING IN TORMENTS, and seeth Abraham
> afar off, and Lazarus in his bosom.**

The rich man in this passage of Scripture didn't go
to hell because he was rich. He went to hell because He
was not *rich toward God.* He left God out of his life and
didn't acknowledge Him as the Author of eternal life.

We read in Luke 16:19-21 that the rich man
"*. . . was clothed in purple and fine linen, and fared
sumptuously every day . . . ,*" while the beggar, Lazarus,
"*. . . was laid at his gate, full of sores. . . desiring to be
fed with the crumbs which fell from the rich man's table.
. . .*" The Bible says Lazarus went to Abraham's bosom
(Paradise) where he was comforted.

But the rich man went to hell, where the Bible says
he "*. . . lift up his eyes, being in torments. . . .*" So we
know from the Bible that there are those people like
this rich man who are tormented in hell today because
they did not acknowledge God in their lives.

Then there's another kind of person who the Bible
says will spend eternity in hell.

> **MATTHEW 25:1-13**
> **1   Then shall the kingdom of heaven be likened
> unto ten virgins, which took their lamps, and went
> forth to meet the bridegroom.**
> **2   And five of them were wise, and five were fool-
> ish.**
> **3   They that were foolish took their lamps, and
> took no oil with them:**
> **4   But the wise took oil in their vessels with their
> lamps.**

5 While the bridegroom tarried, they all slumbered and slept.
6 And at midnight there was a cry made, Behold, the bridegroom cometh; go ye out to meet him.
7 Then all those virgins arose, and trimmed their lamps.
8 And the foolish said unto the wise, Give us of your oil; for our lamps are gone out.
9 But the wise answered, saying, Not so; lest there be not enough for us and you: but go ye rather to them that sell, and buy for yourselves.
10 And while they went to buy, the bridegroom came; and THEY THAT WERE READY went in with him to the marriage: and the door was shut.
11 Afterward came also the other virgins, saying, Lord, Lord, open to us.
12 But he answered and said, Verily I say unto you, I KNOW YOU NOT.
13 Watch therefore, for ye know neither the day nor the hour wherein the Son of man cometh.

Many people have read this parable and have tried to build a doctrine out of it. But you can't build a doctrine on a parable. Usually in a parable there is one main truth the Lord is trying to get over to us. In this passage, it's found in verse 10: *". . . and they that were READY went in with him to the marriage. . . ."* The main truth the Lord wants us to get out of these verses is to be *ready* for Heaven as our eternal destination!

This passage of Scripture is simply talking about being ready. Ready for what? Ready to meet the Master! In this parable there were ten virgins — five were wise and five were foolish. The five foolish virgins weren't bad people. No, they were virgins. They were clean and wholesome, but they just weren't ready to meet the bridegroom. And the Bible says, ". . . *he* [the bridegroom] *answered and said, Verily I say unto you, I KNOW YOU NOT*" (v. 12).

We know that there are people in hell today who were good people, but who just weren't *ready* to meet the Master. They never accepted Jesus Christ as Savior and Lord. Then there are people in hell like the rich man in Luke 16 who behaved wickedly and left God out of their lives.

The Bible also says the fool will be cast into hell.

LUKE 12:16-20
16 And he spake a parable unto them, saying, The ground of a certain rich man brought forth plentifully:
17 And he thought within himself, saying, What shall I do, because I have no room where to bestow my fruits?
18 And he said, This will I do: I will pull down my barns, and build greater; and there will I bestow all my fruits and my goods.
19 And I will say to my soul, Soul, thou hast much goods laid up for many years; take thine ease, eat, drink, and be merry.
20 But God said unto him, THOU FOOL, THIS NIGHT THY SOUL SHALL BE REQUIRED OF THEE: then whose shall those things be, which thou hast provided?

There aren't too many people in the Bible that God called a fool! But you remember in the Old Testament, God says, *"The fool hath said in his heart, There is no God . . . "* (Ps. 14:1). God calls the man who says there

is no God, a fool. And God called the farmer in this
parable a fool.

This farmer's ground brought forth much fruit — so
much fruit that he didn't have any more space to store
all of his goods. This foolish farmer said, *". . . This will
I do: I will pull down my barns, and build greater; and
there will I bestow all my fruits and goods"* (Luke
12:18). So he built even greater barns. Then this foolish
farmer said to himself, *". . . Soul, thou hast much goods
laid up for many years; take thine ease, eat, drink, and
be merry"* (Luke 12:19).

That's the attitude of many in the world today.
Folks are laying up treasures for themselves upon the
earth, and in effect they're saying, "Eat, drink, and be
merry. Just enjoy the pleasures of life today and don't
think about tomorrow." People like that take no thought
whatsoever about eternal things. But God said to this
farmer, *". . . Thou fool, this night thy soul shall be
required of thee: then whose shall those things be, which
thou hast provided?"* (Luke 12:20).

There is a Heaven to gain and a hell to shun. When
I was raised off the bed of sickness, I used to preach in
the school yard and on street corners in the market-
place. I would tell people, "Even if I didn't have a Bible,
I would know there's such a place as hell." I had been
there, you see. And I would tell them the story:

"Why it happened just over at 405 North College
Street," I would tell folks. "It was a Saturday night.
Just as grandpa's clock struck 7:30, my heart stopped.

"I was lying in bed, bedfast. I had been sick all of

my life with a deformed heart and an incurable blood disease. And at 7:30 that night, faster than I can say it, the circulation was cut off in my body, way down at the end of my toes, up to my ankles and my knees, then to my hips and stomach. Then suddenly, I leaped out of my body, like a man would leap off a diving board into a swimming pool.

"As I leaped out of my body I began to descend. It was like going down into a well or a deep cavern. I could look back up through that dark cavern and see the lights on the earth flickering in the distance above me. I was descending feet first — down, down, down — until the lights of the earth completely faded and darkness encompassed me round about.

"It was a darkness so dark, you couldn't see your hand if you held it one inch in front of your face. And the darkness was so dense, it seemed you could cut it with a knife. The further down I went, the darker and hotter it became.

"When I reached the bottom of this cavern of darkness (it took only a few seconds, but it seemed like eternity), I could see fingers of light flickering, as great orange flames of fire crested with white tips played on the wall of blackness.

"At the bottom of the pit was the entrance into hell itself. The pathway that led to hell's gates was a downward incline, and I just sort of floated toward those gates that led to hell, unable to stop my decline. Somehow I knew that once I went through those gates, I could never come back, and I was afraid.

"As I approached the gates of hell, some kind of a creature met me. I kept looking straight ahead, my eyes riveted on hell, so I never looked directly at this creature, but I knew he was there.

"I tried to slow down my descent into those gates, but the creature took me by the arm to escort me in. At that moment, from way above the darkness, a Voice spoke. It was a male Voice, but it was a foreign tongue or language to me. This Voice uttered only a few words, but the entire place — hell itself — shook from top to bottom, like a great earthquake.

"When that Voice spoke, the creature let go of my arm, and I began to float upward, toward the earth and away from hell. It was as if a great suction or magnet drew me upward from my back, and I began to ascend.

"Before I reached the top of the pit, I could see the lights of the earth once again. When I came up from that dark cavern, I was on the front porch at 405 North College Street, just outside the south bedroom. I could see the giant cedar trees there in the yard, and I could see grandpa's porch swing on the porch. Then I seemed to go right through the wall and jump inside my body, like a man would slip his foot inside his boot."

This actually happened three times that night. The third time I began to descend into that darkness, I screamed out in fear, "But God, I belong to the church! I've been baptized in water. I shouldn't be going *down!*" But there was no answer — only the sound of my own voice as my cry echoed through the darkness.

Friends, it takes more than belonging to a church or

being baptized in water to miss hell and go to Heaven. The Bible says, "You must be *born again*" (John 3:3)! You must know Jesus Christ as your own Lord and Savior.

So the third time I came to the bottom of that pit and the creature met me and took me by the arm, that Voice spoke again, and I came floating back to earth. Only this time, as I ascended through the darkness, I began to pray. I began to call on God in the Name of Jesus to save me and to forgive me and cleanse me.

When I leaped back into my body, my natural voice picked up my prayer right in the middle of a sentence and I continued to pray, lying there in my bed. It was 7:40 p.m., so all of this had happened in ten minutes' time. Momma had run outside the first time my heart stopped beating, and she was on the porch praying and calling on God at the top of her voice.

When I came back into my body the third time, she and I were both praying so loudly, they tell me traffic was jammed for two blocks around our house! But I'll tell you, when something like that happens to you, you get serious with God, and you can get loud! Seeing hell will scare you so much, you will want to get right with God! It scared me, and I made Jesus Christ my Lord and Savior that night. When I did, I was transferred out of the kingdom of darkness into the Kingdom of God's Son, Jesus Christ (Col. 1:13)!

Friends, there *is* a Heaven to gain and a hell to shun. You may not be aware of hell today, but when you die, you will spend eternity in either Heaven or hell. And if you don't know Jesus Christ as your personal

Savior, you will go to hell and spend eternity there, in that place of torments and punishment.

But God doesn't want anyone to spend eternity in hell. That's why He sent His Son, Jesus Christ, into the world to die on the Cross and be raised to life again for our redemption. Jesus paid the price with His own blood so that we could be reconciled to God. And it's God's will that every man, woman, boy, and girl accept Jesus Christ as Savior and be saved (1 Tim. 2:4).

I was fortunate to get the opportunity to accept Jesus Christ as my Savior the night my heart stopped three times and I went to hell. If God hadn't spoken as that creature took me by the arm, I would have descended into hell's gates — into hell itself — and that place of torments and punishment would have been my eternal dwelling place.

Because of my experience of going down into that dark place, I've always wanted to tell others there is a Heaven to gain and a hell to shun. I know there's a hell to shun because I've been there. But, really, we should believe there's a hell because *the Bible* says there is. That's what I have endeavored to teach folks all these years — that it's what the Bible says that counts, not someone's opinion.

I was seventeen when I was healed and raised from a deathbed. I had lived with my grandmother most of my childhood. We lived in McKinney, Texas, and my grandmother had a cousin who lived about thirty miles away from us in Sherman, Texas. My grandmother and her cousin would visit each other occasionally.

When I was still bedfast, this cousin, Aunt Lizie, as we called her, would visit us with her daughter, Lorenna. We could never mention God around Aunt Lizie. If we ever did, she would start ranting and raving, saying, "There is no God! There is no Heaven or hell. Every preacher ought to be shot and every church burned down because those preachers are just fooling people. They're just trying to get people's money."

Once Aunt Lizie started ranting and raving, it would take some time for her daughter to get her quieted. When Lorenna eventually got her quiet, we would change the conversation to something else.

Soon after I was healed in 1934, I went into the ministry. Aunt Lizie was up in age before I saw her again about ten years later. I had married by then, and my wife and I were holding a meeting in the town where Aunt Lizie lived. Lorenna, Aunt Lizie's daughter, asked us to come and visit them. There seemed to be such an urgency about her request that we paid Lorenna a visit.

After Lorenna greeted us, she took my hand in hers and began to cry. "Oh, Kenneth. I wanted you to come and talk to Momma. She's living here with me, and she's in a coma. The doctor said she will never recover. If we can get her to come to, will you talk to her?"

"Well, I sure will if I can," I answered her. So Lorenna led us to the bedroom where Aunt Lizie lay in a coma. This dear woman was in her seventies by now, and she was just lying there, dying. Her eyes were wide open, but they were like marbles. She never blinked. Her mouth was partially opened, and there was a rattling sound in her throat as she struggled for breath.

Lorenna leaned over her mother and said, "Momma! Momma!" But there was no answer. "Momma!" Lorenna hollered and shook her a little bit.

Aunt Lizie's mouth stayed partially opened the entire time, but somehow from way down inside, from her throat, Aunt Lizie answered, "Yes, my baby, what is it?" We could hear her plainly, but her lips never moved.

Lorenna said, "Momma, do you remember Aunt Lillie's boy, Kenneth, who was bedfast for so long and later became a preacher?"

When Lorenna said the word "preacher," Aunt Lizie raised herself up in bed, though she never batted an eye and her lips never moved. She reached out her hand to me and said, "Ken! Ken, where are you?" I took her hand, and she said to me, "Oh, Kenneth! Kenneth! You're a preacher. Tell me there's no hell. I said there was no God! I said there was no Heaven, and I said there was no hell!" and Aunt Lizie became frantic.

"Tell me there's no hell," she continued. "I'm so afraid. It's so dark, and I'm so afraid. Oh! Oh!" she gasped, "I'm going to hell!" and Aunt Lizie fell back onto her pillow.

I couldn't tell Aunt Lizie there wasn't a hell. I started to tell her there was a Heaven and that she could go there if she accepted Jesus Christ as her Savior. But Aunt Lizie had exhausted all the strength she had. When she fell back onto her pillow, she lapsed into unconsciousness and never did come out of it. I say it with tears — Aunt Lizie died and went to hell.

So you see, my friends, while you and I sit in our lighted homes here on the earth, many today are in the darkness, misery, and torments of hell. There are people like the rich man we read about in Luke 16 who are in hell today, and they dwell eternally in torments (Luke 16:23). And there are people like the foolish farmer who missed Heaven and went to hell because they valued earthly things more than spiritual things and failed to secure Heaven as their eternal destiny by accepting Jesus Christ as Savior and Lord.

And there are also people in hell today like those five foolish virgins who may have lived good lives but weren't ready to meet the Master because they never accepted Jesus Christ as their Savior. In Matthew 25:12, the bridegroom said to the foolish virgins, ". . . *Verily I say unto you, I KNOW YOU NOT.*" The only accusation brought against them was *they weren't ready to meet the Master, and He didn't know them*!

Are *you* ready to meet the Master? You can be ready if you accept Jesus Christ as your Lord and Savior. The Bible says there is no other name under Heaven but the Name of Jesus by which we can be saved (Acts 4:12).

By accepting Jesus Christ, your name can be written in the Lamb's book of life. Through Jesus, you can miss hell and be listed among the "who's who" of *Heaven* where you will dwell eternally with the Lord!

Chapter 4
A New Creation

Therefore if any man be in Christ, he is a new creature [creation]: *old things are passed away; behold, all things are become new.*
— 2 Corinthians 5:17

Believers, Christians, children of God, I want to talk about *you* for a little while. I want you to notice in God's Word some facts about yourself as a new creation in Christ.

1. *You are a child of God.*

That is not true of everyone in this world. We hear a lot about "the Fatherhood of God and the brotherhood of man." However, Jesus once said to the Pharisees, the most religious people of that day, *"Ye are of your father the devil . . ."* (John 8:44). It is true that God is the Creator of all mankind, but He is only the Father of those who have been born again.

I'm so glad I am a new creature. I was only fifteen when I was born again, but I *knew* when it happened. Something happened on the inside of me in my spirit. It felt like a heavy load weighing at least two tons rolled off my chest.

Not only did that heavy load leave me, but Someone — the Holy Spirit — came *into* me. I was not the same person I had been before. There was a change inside me.

Thank God, as a believer you are a new creation! Your *spirit* has been recreated — not your body. You still have the same body you've always had. But inside your body lives the real you — your spirit man.

Paul calls man's spirit the "inward man," and he calls the body the "outward man": ". . . *though our OUTWARD MAN PERISH, yet the INWARD MAN is RENEWED day by day"* (2 Cor. 4:16). In First Peter 3:4, Peter calls this inner man "the hidden man of the heart." Man's spirit is hidden to the physical eye.

No person can see the real you. No one even knows what the real you looks like. People may think they see you, but they are only looking at the house you live in, your body, the outward man. They don't really see *you.* The real you — your inner man — is on the inside looking out through the windows of your eyes.

As well as you may know someone, you have never seen the real person inside. You only see the house he lives in. When that house in which he lives is decayed, the real man will still live on. His spirit man will never die. Jesus said about Lazarus, ". . . *the beggar died, and* [he] *was carried by the angels into Abraham's bosom . . ."* (Luke 16:22).

It is this inward man who has become a new creation in Christ. He has come into the family of God. He is a child of God. He is in perfect union with the Master.

2. *You are one with the Master.*

The believer and Jesus are one. God's Word declares, *"But he that is joined unto the Lord is ONE SPIRIT"* (1 Cor. 6:17).

Jesus said, "I am the vine, you are the branches" (John 15:5). As you look at a tree, you don't think of the branches as being separate from the rest of the tree. When you look at the tree and its branches, you see them as one — a single entity. In the same way, we are one with Christ. Our spirits are joined to Him. Jesus is the Head, and we are His Body.

3. *All things are possible to you.*

If I quoted the scriptures which say, ". . . *with God all things are possible*" (Matt. 19:26; Mark 10:27), everyone would readily agree that God can do all things. However, the same Bible that says, "all things are possible with God," also says, ". . . *all things are possible TO HIM THAT BELIEVETH*" (Mark 9:23).

Is the second verse as true as the first verse? Of course. Could the first verse be a statement of fact and the second one be a misconception or a falsehood? No! They are *both* statements of fact.

All things are possible to him that believes! It helps me sometimes as I drive down the road to say that aloud. It helps me if I am facing a seemingly impossible situation to say aloud to myself, "All things are possible to him that believes — and I believe!"

One translation reads, "All things are possible to a believing one." I quote that aloud and then add, "I am a believing one."

4. *The Greater One is in you.*

1 JOHN 4:4
4 Ye are of God, little children, and have over-

come them: because **GREATER IS HE THAT IS IN YOU, than he that is in the world.**

This verse is true concerning *you.* You may not be taking advantage of it, but it is still true. It is yours.

Notice the phrase, "Ye are of God." That is another way of saying you are born of God. John is saying the same thing Paul said in Second Corinthians 5:17: *". . . if any man be in Christ, he is a new creature. . . ."* John is telling us that we are *born of God* — that our spirits have been *recreated* or *born again.*

It's sad to say, but many believers really do not know they have been born of God in the new birth and have received eternal life. They think eternal life is something they are *going* to have when they get to Heaven.

Many believers simply think they have received forgiveness of sins. They have only been taught that their sins have been forgiven and that they must be very careful in their Christian walk in order to remain justified before God. They've never been taught that *the nature of God resides in their spirits.* No one ever told them that they are actually new creations in Christ. And because of their ignorance on this subject, sin and Satan continue to reign over them.

But when believers understand that the man on the inside, the real man, has been born again and is a new creation in Christ Jesus, they can begin to live according to the power of the Greater One who lives in them. Then they can begin to rule over sin and Satan in their lives, instead of the devil ruling over *them.*

Because of Jesus' mighty triumph over Satan at the Cross, we, too, can live in triumph over the devil. Thank God, greater is He that is in us than Satan, the god of this world! The Greater One is greater than demons and evil spirits. He is greater than sickness and greater than disease. And He lives in me! He lives in you! He that is in us is greater than *any* force we may come against.

When John wrote about the Greater One living inside us, he was writing to born-again, Spirit-filled believers. I maintain that all born-again, Spirit-filled believers have within them, ready for use, all the power and ability they will ever need to put them over. We are thoroughly prepared for any emergency that may come *because the Greater One is in us.*

2 CORINTHIANS 6:16
16 . . . for ye are the temple of the living God; as God hath said, I WILL DWELL IN THEM, and walk in them; and I will be their God, and they shall be my people.

How many of us are conscious of the fact that God is dwelling in us? It sounds far-fetched. But what does this scripture mean if it doesn't mean what it says? Our natural minds may have a hard time grasping it, but the truth is, the Bible emphatically declares that believers ". . . *are the temple of the living God . . .*" (2 Cor. 6:16).

Notice First John 4:4 says, ". . . *greater is HE that is*

in you. . . ." He — the Holy Spirit — is a divine Personality, not just an influence or an impersonal being. Jesus said, *". . . I will pray the Father, and he shall give you another Comforter, that HE* [the Holy Spirit] *may abide with you for ever"* (John 14:16). God the Father, in the Person and power of the Holy Ghost, indwells us! He lives *in* us!

It is time for the Church to become "God-inside" minded. For too long the Church has been weakness-minded, sickness-minded, inferiority-minded, trouble-minded, and poverty-minded.

Do you realize what we've done? Often we've been so negative-minded that that is all we *have* minded! For too long the negative side of life is all many of us have thought about and talked about.

This negative thinking has created a very serious condition of doubt, unbelief, and spiritual failure in the Church and in the believer. The Church has operated more or less on a psychology of unbelief, which has robbed believers of vibrant Christian faith and living. It has robbed us of the abundant life Jesus intended us to have. Jesus said, *"The thief cometh not, but for to steal, and to kill, and to destroy: I am come that they might have LIFE, and that they might have it MORE ABUNDANTLY"* (John 10:10).

When we really understand that the Life-Giver indwells us — that Jesus, the Author of all life, condescended to come down and live in us in the Person and power of the Holy Ghost — then our very being will radiate God's life.

So we must become life-minded, not death-minded. The Bible says, ". . . *God hath given to us eternal life, and this life is in his Son*" (1 John 5:11).

We must become plenty-minded, not poverty-minded. God is a God of plenty (Joel 2:26).

We must become health-minded, not sickness-minded. God said, ". . . *I am the Lord that healeth thee*" (Exod. 15:26).

We must become deliverance-minded, not trouble-minded. God said, ". . . *I will be with him in trouble; I will deliver him . . .*" (Ps. 91:15). God never promised we wouldn't have any trouble. But He did promise to be with us in trouble and to deliver us.

We must become power-minded, not weakness-minded. The Holy Ghost — the divine Power House and the Source of all power — indwells us, and the potential of all His power resides within us.

PHILIPPIANS 2:13
13 For it is God which worketh IN YOU both to will and to do of his good pleasure.

Another translation reads, "For it is God who is at work within you. . . ." I like to put that together with First John 4:4: ". . . *greater is he that is in you . . .*" and make the confession, "Greater is He that is working in *me*."

God is in me by the Holy Spirit! What is He doing in me? He is at work inside me. What is He working at? He is causing me both to will and to do His good pleasure. What is His own good pleasure? It's His good pleasure that I have everything the Word of God says I can have. It's His good pleasure that I do everything God's Word says I can do.

The Greater One is enabling me! He is in me, and my spirit rejoices. My heart is glad because I know I can turn Him loose in me. I can let Him have the right-of-way in me. I can put Him to work to an even greater degree in my life.

How can you put the Greater One to work in your life? First you must *believe in your heart* that the Holy Spirit is in you and that the Word of God is true. Then you must boldly *confess the Word with your mouth*, for you will not enjoy the reality of what *the Word* states is yours until you confess it. You will not possess what you believe *in your heart* according to God's Word until you confess it.

The Bible teaches, ". . . *with the HEART man BELIEVETH . . . and with the MOUTH CONFESSION is made . . .*" (Rom. 10:10). Your confession should be that the Holy Spirit is at work *within* you, and that He works *through* you.

In the new birth, God recreates us, making us His own children. The moment we are born again, the Holy Ghost comes in and lives in us. Through the Holy Spirit, God imparts unto our spirits eternal life, which is God's nature.

1 CORINTHIANS 6:19
19 What? know ye not that your body is the temple of the Holy Ghost which is in you, which ye have of God, and ye are not your own?

Our bodies have become the temple of God. God indwells us. Then He ministers through us to the world and to the Church. He ministers through the words we speak. He ministers through us as we lay our hands on the sick.

Greater is He that is *in you* than he that is in the world (1 John 4:4). Grasp that fact today as never before. You are of God. You are born from above. The same mighty Spirit that raised the body of Jesus Christ from the dead dwells in you.

Can you see why Jesus said, "... *all things are possible to him that believeth*" (Mark 9:23)? Jesus said that because the God with whom all things are possible lives within us!

How abundant life becomes when we begin to understand what it means to live as new creations in Christ! How limitless ministry becomes when we finally realize the integrity of the Word, and when we *know* that we are who God says we are, and we can do what God says we can do in His Word!

Chapter 5
Understanding Righteousness

For with the heart man BELIEVETH unto RIGHTEOUSNESS. . . .
— Romans 10:10

For if by one man's offence death reigned by one; much more they which receive abundance of grace and of THE GIFT OF RIGHTEOUSNESS shall reign in life by one, Jesus Christ.
— Romans 5:17

We glean two significant facts about righteousness from these verses:

1. With the heart man *believes* unto righteousness.

2. Righteousness is a *gift*.

Righteousness means *right standing with God*. We have right standing with God, not because of what *we* did, but because of what Jesus did for us in God's great plan of redemption. The newborn babe in Christ has as good a standing with God and can get an answer to prayer just as quickly as the mature saint who has lived many years for God.

Too often we associate righteousness with good works. The Bible teaches that good works and right conduct are important, of course. But all our good works and all our right conduct could never make us righteous. If they could, we wouldn't need Jesus.

We've mistakenly thought we might somehow grow into righteousness. Thank God, we can grow in the Lord and can develop spiritually. But righteousness is not something we can work to attain. We cannot grow into righteousness; it's a *gift* from God.

If you have been born again, you will never be more righteous than you are now. You won't be any more righteous when you get to Heaven than you are at this moment.

How do you become righteous? By *believing* unto righteousness (Rom. 10:10) and *receiving* the *gift* of righteousness (Rom. 5:17).

When you were born again, you became a new man in Christ Jesus — a new creation — and you were made the righteousness of God in Him (2 Cor. 5:17). In the new birth, you were born righteous!

> **ROMANS 3:21,22**
> 21 But now **THE RIGHTEOUSNESS OF GOD** without the law **IS MANIFESTED,** being witnessed by the law and the prophets;
> 22 Even the **RIGHTEOUSNESS OF GOD** which is **BY FAITH OF JESUS CHRIST** unto all and upon ALL them that BELIEVE. . . .

In His great plan of redemption, God made provision for all who believe in Jesus to have right standing before Him. That sets something to dancing inside me!

It's so important for believers to understand that they have been made righteous in Christ. A lack of understanding of righteousness holds more people in bondage than perhaps anything else. In my opinion, righteousness is one of the most misunderstood subjects in the Bible.

In my own personal experience, not understanding righteousness almost cost me my life. At sixteen years of age, five doctors gave me up to die. But my spirit kept telling me I didn't have to die. (Your spirit knows things your head doesn't, particularly if your spirit is born of God.) My heart told me there was hope and help in God's Word.

So while I was bedfast and almost totally paralyzed, I studied the Word, endeavoring to keep an open mind. As I did, I began to see some truths about faith and prayer. And when I saw those great statements that were spoken by Jesus in Mark 11:23 and 24, my spirit leaped with joy within me.

Thrilled, I decided to run a reference on scriptures pertaining to faith and prayer. That brought me to James chapter 5.

> **JAMES 5:14,15**
> **14 Is any SICK among you? LET HIM CALL FOR THE ELDERS OF THE CHURCH; and let them pray over him, anointing him with oil in the name of the Lord:**
> **15 And THE PRAYER OF FAITH SHALL SAVE THE SICK, and the Lord shall raise him up; and if he have committed sins, they shall be forgiven him.**

When I read that the sick were to call for the elders

of the church, tears sprang to my eyes. I thought a person *had* to do that to be healed, and I didn't know of any church elders I could call who believed in divine healing.

Then the Holy Spirit, who is our Teacher, spoke to me and called something to my attention. (When I say the Holy Spirit spoke to me, I mean it was as though someone spoke up from inside me, within my spirit.)

The Holy Spirit said, "Did you notice that James 5:15 says, '. . . *the prayer of faith shall save the sick* . . .'?"

I read it again. "Yes," I answered, "it does say that."

"You can pray that prayer as well as anyone," the Voice within me said.

I began to see what the Holy Ghost was telling me! I began to believe it!

But then I read a little further, and I stumbled on the very next verse.

JAMES 5:16
16 Confess your faults one to another, and pray one for another, that ye may be healed. The effectual fervent prayer of A RIGHTEOUS MAN availeth much.

When I read that, the devil took advantage of my lack of understanding to defeat me. He knew I didn't know the meaning of righteousness.

"Well, yes," the devil said, "you *could* pray the prayer of faith and receive your healing — *if* you were righteous. You see it says in James 5:16, '. . . *The effectual fervent prayer of a RIGHTEOUS man availeth much.*'"

When Satan spoke to me, it was like a voice speaking in my mind. Notice Satan didn't contradict what the Holy Spirit had said to me. The devil didn't say, "You *can't* pray the prayer of faith." He knew I believed I *could* pray in faith.

So instead, the devil looked for another way to defeat me. He reminded me of my past mistakes and failures by putting mental pictures of them in my mind.

"Can you really say you're righteous?" he asked. Not understanding what righteousness is, I examined myself from the natural standpoint. In light of my past sins and failures, I was definitely not what I considered righteous. So my answer was, "No, I can't."

Then I began to reason in my mind: *If I could just live long enough, maybe I could develop enough spiritually to become righteous. And according to James 5:16, if I ever do become righteous, I'll be a whiz when it comes to praying.*

I laid the whole subject of righteousness aside because I was certain I didn't qualify. My ignorance regarding righteousness allowed Satan to rob me of my healing at that time — something that God had already provided for me and wanted me to have right then.

Months later while I was still bedfast, the next verse in this passage in James 5 caught my attention.

JAMES 5:17,18
17 Elias [Elijah] was a man subject to like passions as we are, and he prayed earnestly that it might not rain: and it rained not on the earth by the space of three years and six months.

18 And he prayed again, and the heaven gave rain, and the earth brought forth her fruit.

I thought, *If Elijah is given as an example of a righteous man who prayed and got results, I'll study about him in the Bible. Then I can follow his example and get results to my prayers.*

But the more I read about Elijah, the more he reminded me of myself. Actually, that's just what James meant when he said in effect, "Elijah was a man just like us. He was subject to the same human thoughts and emotions that we are."

Elijah did have his great moments. He prayed and kept rain from falling for three years (1 Kings 17:1). He prayed down fire from Heaven (1 Kings 18:36-38). He slew the prophets of Baal (1 Kings 18:40). He prayed down rain in the midst of a three-year drought (1 Kings 18:42-45). The Spirit of God came on him and he outran the king's chariot fourteen miles across the plains of Jezreel (1 Kings 18:46).

But when he got to Jezreel someone told him, "Jezebel said that by this time tomorrow, she's going to make sure you're dead." Elijah started running again (1 Kings 19:2,3). But this time the hand of the Lord wasn't upon him. It was just Elijah running in fear.

Elijah ran until he was too tired to run anymore. Then he sat down under a juniper tree and cried, "Lord, just let me die" (1 Kings 19:4).

Elijah didn't really want to die. If he had really wanted to die, why didn't he just stay where he was?

Jezebel would have made sure he died! Why go to the trouble of running all that distance and *then* die?

No, Elijah didn't want to die any more than a person does when out of frustration he says, "I might as well be dead." You see, Elijah was a man subject to like passions as we are.

"Lord," Elijah said, "You might as well let me die. I'm the only one left anyway. Everyone else is backslidden but me."

There are folks today who say, "No one else has the truth except me and my little bunch." I'm so glad they're wrong!

God had to correct Elijah. "No, I have seven thousand reserved unto Myself who have not bowed their knees to Baal" (1 Kings 19:18).

As I read about Elijah in the Old Testament, I thought, *How could God call Elijah righteous? He's not my idea of a righteous man.* (We get in trouble when we substitute our ideas for God's Word.) *Yet James inspired by the Holy Spirit gave him as an example of a righteous man praying!*

I continued to study the Word as I lay on the bed of sickness. Then I discovered Psalm 32.

> **PSALM 32:1,2**
> 1 **Blessed is he whose transgression is forgiven, whose sin is covered.**
> 2 **Blessed is the man unto whom the Lord imputeth not iniquity....**

I came to realize that under the Old Covenant, God

set up a system whereby the blood of innocent animals could be shed to cover the sins of His people. Then God did not *impute* iniquity unto the Israelites; He imputed righteousness unto them. That means He *counted* them as righteous.

I began to see that in the New Testament we have a better covenant established on better promises (Heb. 8:6). Our sins are not *covered*; we are *cleansed* from sin by the blood of our Lord Jesus Christ (1 John 1:7,9).

> **2 CORINTHIANS 5:17,21**
> **17 Therefore if any man be in Christ, he is a new creature: old things are passed away; behold, all things are become new. . . .**
> **21 For he hath made him to be sin for us, who knew no sin; that WE MIGHT BE MADE THE RIGHTEOUSNESS OF GOD in him.**

In Christ we have become new creatures. In Him we have become the righteousness of God.

When I saw that Satan had tried to defeat me through my lack of knowledge about righteousness, I began to say, "I am the righteousness of God in Christ. I am that righteous man James talked about whose prayer avails much. And I am a whiz at praying!" And I soon got off that bed and walked away healed!

If you are in Christ, you can be a whiz at praying too. The effectual, fervent prayer of a righteous man avails *much* (James 5:16). Take advantage of the power that's available through prayer. That power doesn't work automatically without your doing anything. It is knowledge *acted upon* that brings results.

Take your place in prayer as a righteous believer in Christ. Know this: God will hear you pray just as quickly as he hears anyone else pray. You have as good a standing with God as any preacher or minister or any other believer. God will hear and answer your effectual, fervent prayer of faith!

Let's look at Romans 5:17 again.

ROMANS 5:17
17 For if by one man's offence death reigned by one; much more they which receive abundance of grace and of the gift of righteousness shall REIGN IN LIFE by one, Jesus Christ.

The *Amplified* translation says, "reign as *kings*." In the days of Paul, there were many kings ruling over earthly domains. In a king's domain, his word was the final authority. Whatever he said, people obeyed! He *reigned*.

God's Word says *we* shall reign. Where? In this life. How? By Christ Jesus because we have been made the righteousness of God in Christ.

Jesus, who is altogether righteous, became *our* righteousness. Our standing with God is secure. Therefore we can stand in the Presence of God as though we had never sinned. We can stand in God's Presence without a sense of condemnation or an inferiority complex.

No wonder the Word says, *"Let us therefore come boldly unto the throne of grace, that we may obtain mercy, and find grace to help in time of need"* (Heb. 4:16). It's all because of Jesus!

In this life, every one of us will face the attacks of the enemy. But we can stand before the devil without fear. He cannot condemn us when we've already been made righteous.

When you know the truth of your right standing in Jesus, you can stand in Satan's presence with the authority given to you in the Name of Jesus and exercise dominion over the devil, demons, and disease. You'll know you stand righteous in Jesus, and nothing can by any means harm you (Luke 10:19).

By gaining a revelation of your righteous standing before God in Christ, you can step out of the narrow place of religious tradition and sin-consciousness into the boundless fullness of God!

Chapter 6

Seven Fundamental Principles For Spiritual Growth

To grow spiritually, there are seven steps you must take. If you do not take these steps, whatever else you do, you will be a failure when it comes to spiritual development. These steps are elementary. I call them the seven fundamental principles for spiritual growth.

Step One: Learn To Forget

Step one in spiritual development is *to learn to forget the past.*

> **PHILIPPIANS 3:13,14**
> **13 Brethren, I count not myself to have apprehended: but this one thing I do, FORGETTING THOSE THINGS WHICH ARE BEHIND, and reaching forth unto those things which are before,**
> **14 I press toward the mark for the prize of the high calling of God in Christ Jesus.**

To grow spiritually, you must do the things Paul suggests in these verses. Notice Paul doesn't believe he has "arrived" yet. He says he is still pressing toward the mark. The person who thinks he has arrived and knows it all will never grow spiritually. Nobody knows it all!

Actually, the more you grow in the Lord and learn about Him, the more you realize how little you know.

For example, I don't know nearly as much as I used to think I knew! The more spiritually immature I was, the more I thought I knew.

Before you can press toward the mark for the prize of the high calling of God in Christ Jesus, you must take the first step of spiritual development by *". . . forgetting those things which are behind"* (Phil. 3:13). You'll never be a successful Christian unless your "forgetter" is in good working order.

Forget even the blessings of God that are behind, because if you live on past blessings, you are living on stale manna. If you're satisfied with what happened in the past, you are not reaching toward the future blessings God has in store for you.

Smith Wigglesworth said, "I am satisfied only with the dissatisfaction that has to be satisfied again and again." Wigglesworth meant that no matter what blessings of God he had known, or what spiritual plateau he had attained, he was still dissatisfied. He always wanted more of God.

Let us never come to the place where we say, "I'm satisfied with my knowledge of God." Thank God for His blessings and for the spiritual experiences we've had in the past. But let us be like Wigglesworth, and only be satisfied with the dissatisfaction that has to be satisfied again and again. Otherwise we will stop growing spiritually.

There is another side of learning to forget that is important: *You must learn to forget your past mistakes, failures, and sins.* As long as Satan can keep those past failures before you, he holds you in a position where you will not develop spiritually, and your prayers and faith will not work.

All of us have failed. We're not proud of it. We're not advertising it. But all of us have failed in one way or another more often than we'd like to admit.

As you grow spiritually and look back at the times you thought you were doing well, you'll discover you weren't doing as well as you thought you were. I found this out when I would reflect on how well I did as a pastor. When I left a church, often I thought I had done a good job; in some cases, I even thought I had done a *superb* job.

But a year or two later, with a little more growth and maturity, I almost hid my face so people wouldn't see me blushing, I was so embarrassed. I found out I had come up short and had even sinned without realizing it.

We are to confess those sins we know about. But sins we don't know about or are ignorant of are perpetually cleansed by the blood of Jesus as we appropriate the saving grace of His blood in our lives.

ISAIAH 43:25
25 I, even I, am he that blotteth out thy transgressions for mine own sake, and WILL NOT REMEMBER THY SINS.

The writer of the Book of Hebrews makes a similar statement: *"For I will be merciful to their unrighteousness, and their sins and THEIR INIQUITIES WILL I*

REMEMBER NO MORE" (Heb. 8:12).

The Word of God is the cure for sin-consciousness. Hallelujah, He's forgotten our past sins! No wonder the Bible says, *"Let us therefore come boldly unto the throne of grace, that we may obtain mercy, and find grace to help in time of need"* (Heb. 4:16).

John wrote the Book of First John to the Church, not to the world. He was talking to believers when he said, *"If we confess our sins, he is faithful and just to forgive us our sins, and to cleanse us from all unrighteousness"* (1 John 1:9).

Thank God for His promise of forgiveness! That verse doesn't belong to the sinner. That's not a confession the sinner can make. A sinner couldn't remember everything he has done wrong because his whole nature is wrong since his spirit hasn't been born again. No, John wrote this verse to Christians.

God does not want us to sin. But if we do, Jesus Christ is our Advocate with the Father to plead our case.

1 JOHN 2:1,2
1 My little children, these things write I unto you, that ye sin not. And if any man sin, we have an advocate with the Father, Jesus Christ the righteous:
2 And he is the propitiation for our sins: and not for ours only, but also for the sins of the whole world.

John is saying that Jesus is the atonement for our sins, as well as for the sins of the whole world.

When we put all these scriptures together, they tell us that when we confess our sins, God not only *cleanses* us from all unrighteousness and forgives us, but He *will not remember* our sins anymore.

In order to grow spiritually, every believer needs to take advantage of First John 1:9 and First John 2:1,2 to receive forgiveness for his sins. However, once a believer confesses his sin, he must make the decision to stop remembering them because God forgets them!

So forget what the Lord has forgotten. Forget what is behind. If you think about it, it will hinder your spiritual progress. It will keep your faith and prayers from working. It can keep you from receiving healing for your body and other blessings and provisions of God.

Step Two: Learn To Forgive

Step two in spiritual development is closely associated with learning to forget the past. If you want to grow spiritually, you must also *learn to forgive*.

EPHESIANS 4:32
32 And be ye kind one to another, tenderhearted, FORGIVING ONE ANOTHER, EVEN AS God for Christ's sake hath forgiven you.

It's easy to be kind to those who are kind to you. It's easy to be tenderhearted toward people who are tenderhearted toward you. It's not so easy to be kind to those who treat you badly. But notice Paul said, "Be kind to one another even as God forgave you." That means you have to forgive fellow believers too.

How did God say He forgives? In Isaiah 43:25 He said, "I will blot out your transgressions and I will not remember your sins anymore." To forgive as God forgives means you are not to remember any wrong a fellow Christian might have done to you.

I've seen people get sick and stay sick because they didn't practice this verse of Scripture. By refusing to be kind and tenderhearted, they became hard-hearted and unforgiving, and it poisoned their physical body. On the other hand, I've seen people get healed just as soon as they made an adjustment by choosing to forgive others. They didn't even need prayer for healing.

Jesus gave us the classic text on God's forgiveness in Matthew 18. This is God's law of forgiveness:

> **MATTHEW 18:21,22**
> **21 Then came Peter to him, and said, Lord, how oft shall my brother sin against me, and I forgive Him? till seven times?**
> **22 Jesus saith unto him, I say not unto thee, Until seven times: but, Until SEVENTY TIMES SEVEN.**

That's 490 times!

I've had people say to me, "Yes, but you don't know what So-and-so did to me!"

It doesn't matter what anyone has done to any of us. It couldn't come close to the debt we owe the Lord for forgiving our sins. How much more should we be willing to have pity on others — especially on our brothers and sisters in Christ!

When you learn God's law of forgiveness, you will grow spiritually!

Step Three: Learn To Pray

Step three in spiritual development is *to learn how to pray*. You cannot grow spiritually and be a success in your Christian walk without developing a prayer life.

A successful prayer life must be built upon the Word of God. In John 15:7, Jesus said, *"If YE ABIDE IN ME, and MY WORDS ABIDE IN YOU, ye shall ask what ye will, and it shall be done unto you."*

If you took part of that verse out of its setting, and read, *". . . ye shall ask what ye will, and it shall be done unto you,"* you would say, "Goody, goody! Isn't that wonderful? He said I could ask whatever I want, and it would be done for me. 'Lord, I want this' and 'Lord, I want that.' And I'll get it because I've asked."

But wait a minute. That's not what Jesus said. Don't run off with just a part of that verse and begin asking God for everything you can think of. Asking what you will and having it done for you is conditional on the rest of the verse: *"If ye abide in me. . . ."* To abide in Jesus means not only to be born again, but to walk in *continual fellowship* with Him.

Look at the other conditional part of that verse: *". . . and my words abide in you. . . ."* You'll never be successful in your prayer life if you don't know God's Word. God's Word must *abide* or *live* in your heart.

When people ask me to agree in prayer with them

about something, I ask them if they know what the Word of God says on the matter. Then I ask them if they are standing in faith for the situation. I ask, "What scriptures are you standing on?" Too often they reply, "Not any in particular." I tell them, "Well, then, that's what you'll get — nothing in particular!"

You'll only receive answers to your prayers when your prayer life is built on the Word of God. So when you have a need, find scriptures that promise you what you're praying about. Then you will have a solid foundation for your faith.

I'll be honest with you. Certain needs have arisen in my life, in my family, or in my ministry that I didn't pray about right away. Sometimes I didn't pray about them for several days.

I wanted to pray in faith about the matter and have it settled once and for all. So I took time to get into the Word first and build a solid foundation for my faith. Even though I already knew what the Word said on the subject, I took time to once again establish the Word in my heart so I would have a solid foundation for my faith.

God already told me in His Word that the answer to my prayer is part of my inheritance in Christ. Therefore, I knew I didn't have to come to prayer with an "if." The answer already belonged to me! I could just pray, ask Him for that need to be met, and then keep praising Him for the answer until the manifestation came.

If you cannot find specific scriptures that promise to meet your need, then ask God to talk to you about your situation. The Bible promises, *"For as many as are led*

by the Spirit of God, they are the sons of God" (Rom.
8:14). As you wait on God in faith, the Holy Spirit will
minister God's wisdom to you from His Word about your
situation. Of course, the Holy Spirit's guidance will
always be in line with the Word.

Once you have a foundation for faith in the Word,
then pray according to the scriptural guidelines Jesus
gave us for New Testament prayer. That's part of allowing God's words to abide in you.

> **JOHN 16:23,24**
> **23 And in that day ye shall ask me nothing. Verily,
> verily, I say unto you, Whatsoever ye shall ASK
> THE FATHER IN MY NAME, he will give it you.
> 24 Hitherto have ye asked nothing in my name:
> ask, and ye shall receive, that your joy may be full.**

Pray *to the Father* in the *Name of Jesus.* That is the
divine order for New Testament praying.

It's only as you build your prayer life solidly on the
Word of God that you can grow spiritually.

Step Four: Learn To Believe

Step four in spiritual development is closely associated with learning to pray. You must also *learn to
believe* God and His Word.

The prayer of faith just won't work unless you
believe. How do you believe? It's simple. Jesus said in
Mark 11:24: *". . . What things soever ye desire, when ye
pray, BELIEVE that ye RECEIVE them, and ye shall
have them."*

We often fail to receive what we've asked for because we walk *by sight* instead of *by faith* in the promises of God. We say, "When it comes to pass — when I can *see* I have it — *then* I'll believe it."

But that's the "Thomas" kind of faith! Thomas said, "... *EXCEPT I SHALL SEE in his hands the print of the nails, and put my finger into the print of the nails, and thrust my hand into his side, I WILL NOT BELIEVE*" (John 20:25).

On the other hand, we can walk by the "Abraham" kind of faith. The Bible says that Abraham "... *against hope believed in hope* ... *according to that which was spoken. ... And being not weak in faith, he considered not his own body ...*" (Rom. 4:18,19). Abraham "considered not" the natural circumstances. He believed he had received God's promise many years before he actually saw the answer to his prayer and his wife bore him a son.

Believe that you receive *when you pray*, and you will have it. It's the most difficult thing in the world to make people understand this, because they are usually so bound up in the sense realm with human reasoning. Most people want to have their answer *first*, and then they will believe they have received it.

Even wonderful, born-again, Spirit-filled, consecrated and dedicated people are often not motivated by *biblical* faith — walking by the promises in God's Word. Sometimes even ministers of the gospel, whom I esteem highly and who love me, tell me, "I just can't go along with that faith business you preach."

Or some ministers say, "Yes, Kenneth is a good fellow, all right. But he's off on a tangent preaching faith." Well, if I am, I'm out there with Jesus and the Word of God. I'm just preaching what the Bible says. I didn't write the Bible — God did!

Jesus is the One who said, ". . . *What things soever ye desire, when ye pray, believe that ye receive them, and ye shall have them*" (Mark 11:24). I didn't write that verse; I just believe it! Why add to or take away from the Word of God? Why not just take it for what it says?

Believing according to the Word requires a conscious decision to live beyond your five senses. Faith is a *sixth* sense, so to speak. Faith is believing God's Word in your *heart* or *spirit*. That's what Jesus said in Mark 11:23: ". . . *Whosoever . . . shall not doubt IN HIS HEART, but SHALL BELIEVE* [in his heart] *that those things which he saith shall come to pass; he shall have whatsoever he saith.*" Believe where? In his *heart*.

You see, your head will fight you if it hasn't been renewed sufficiently with the Word of God. Your own mental thinking will try to keep you in the natural realm. But if you'll just persist in believing God's Word in your heart, you'll grow strong in faith. And no matter what your head tells you, you'll get results. The Bible says so. I know from experience. I've proven the Word to be so time after time in the midst of tremendous opposition.

If you want to grow spiritually, you must learn to believe God's Word regardless of natural circumstances.

Step Five: Learn To Worship

Step five in spiritual development is *to learn to worship*.

In John 4, Jesus said to the Samaritan woman at the well: *"But the hour cometh, and now is, when the true worshippers shall WORSHIP the Father IN SPIRIT AND IN TRUTH: for the Father seeketh such to worship him. God is a Spirit: and they that worship him must worship him in spirit and in truth"* (John 4:23,24).

Hallelujah! That means you don't have to be in a particular place to worship God. A lot of people think you can't worship God unless you are in a church building.

God doesn't dwell in buildings anymore. Under the Old Covenant, He used to dwell in the Holy of Holies in the Temple. But under the New Covenant He dwells in *us*. Our bodies — not some brick-and-mortar building — have become the temple of the living God (1 Cor. 3:16). So learn to worship God with your spirit, not in some dead, formal way with your mental faculties or your soul.

The Lord has enabled us to worship Him in Spirit and in truth because the Holy Spirit dwells in us. Also, by speaking in tongues we have a supernatural means of communicating with Him (1 Cor. 14:2).

Paul said in First Corinthians 14:2: *"For he that speaketh in an unknown tongue speaketh not unto men, but unto God: for no man understandeth him; howbeit in the spirit he speaketh mysteries." Moffatt*'s translation says, ". . . he is talking of divine secrets in the Spirit."

Thank God for this wonderful means of communicating with the Father! We need times of prayer when we get alone with God and worship Him in other tongues, as well as with our understanding in our native tongue.

However, you may use all the adjectives at your disposal in your native language to tell God how wonderful He is, but your words will not suffice. But when you begin to fellowship with Him in that supernatural language, some way or another your heart finds satisfaction. Your spirit is in direct contact with the Father of spirits — the Father of our Lord Jesus Christ — and your spirit is able to express your deepest innermost thoughts and feelings.

Take time to worship God. Learning to worship Him will help you grow spiritually.

Step Six: Learn To Give

Step six in spiritual development is *to learn the secret of giving*. The church needs a general overhaul on this subject to keep from becoming unbalanced.

Some people have gone to one extreme in their giving. They only give because they feel it's their duty or obligation (which, of course, it is). But because that's the only reason they give into the Kingdom of God, they miss the blessing giving can be in their lives.

You should give to the Lord because you love Him,

worship Him, and adore Him. And you need to add faith to your giving. Tell the Lord you are mixing faith with your giving, and remind Him of the scripture: *"Give, and it shall be given unto you; good measure, pressed down, and shaken together, and running over, shall men give into your bosom. For with the same measure that ye mete withal it shall be measured to you again"* (Luke 6:38).

On the other hand, you can go to the other extreme. You can give selfishly just to get a return — and you won't get one.

Some people hear a faith teacher relate how he gave away an automobile and God gave him another one. Then they give theirs away and think, *Now God is going to give me a new car.* But He won't. You see, their motive is all wrong. It's selfish. And it's based on another person's *experience*, not on the *Word*.

You've got to examine your motives for giving and keep your motives right. You can do the right thing with the wrong motive, and it won't work.

Certainly I expect God to keep His Word when I give. And He will, too, if I fulfill my part of the obligation. But I'm not going to give away my automobile just because someone else did. I would only give it away if the Lord told me to. Then because I obeyed God, He would bless my obedience.

We need balance in this area of giving. If we'll keep our motives pure and give according to the Word and the Holy Spirit's leading, we'll be blessed in our own lives and we'll grow in our Christian walk.

Step Seven: Learn To Witness

Step seven in spiritual development is *to learn to witness for the Lord.*

Jesus stated that believers were to receive the baptism of the Holy Spirit so they could become witnesses for Him. That was one of the purposes of the endowment of power from on high: *"But ye shall RECEIVE POWER, after that the Holy Ghost is come upon you: and YE SHALL BE WITNESSES UNTO ME . . ."* (Acts 1:8).

I am thoroughly convinced that the greatest witness you can be to the world is to live a life that's sold out to the Lord. Like the old proverb says, "What you are speaks so loud, I can't hear what you say."

I believe in personally witnessing to people, of course. I think we should witness as the need arises. But I don't think we should go around trying to push the gospel off on everyone. I think we should be led by the Holy Spirit when we witness to other people about the Lord. Otherwise we'll waste our time, and they won't be open to what we're saying.

Smith Wigglesworth purposed to lead at least one soul to God every day. In those days he was working as a plumber in a large city. But during his lunch hour, he would stand on a street corner and pray, "Lord, lead me to the right person." He would wait for the leading of the Spirit. When Wigglesworth sensed the Holy Spirit's nudge, he would follow the Lord's leading, and he would always win the person to the Lord.

You see, the Lord knows who is open to the gospel and who isn't. If you don't wait for His leading, you will do a lot of laboring and never win anyone to the Lord. And many people won't appreciate your efforts. You might even do more harm than good.

In regard to my own mother, brothers, and sister, I never said a word to them about God and the Bible. I never invited one of them to come and hear me preach, even when I was preaching in the same town where they lived. I never said a word to them about Jesus. Not once. (I did to other people, but not to them.)

I just believed if my family could see I had something real, they would want it. And do you know what? Every single one of them followed me into salvation. Every one of them were saved and filled with the Holy Spirit.

I believe the greatest witnessing tool is a life really lived for the Lord. So learn to witness as you are led by the Holy Spirit. But first and foremost, *be* a witness. It's important to your spiritual growth.

So apply yourself to learn these seven fundamental principles for spiritual growth. And don't get frustrated because you won't grow up spiritually overnight. Just take it a step at a time. As you learn to *forget*, to *forgive*, to *pray*, to *believe*, to *worship*, to *give*, and to *witness*, you will be well on your way to spiritual maturity!

Chapter 7
God's Recipe
For Life and Health

> *My son, ATTEND TO MY WORDS; incline thine ear unto my sayings.*
>
> *Let them not depart from thine eyes; keep them in the midst of thine heart.*
>
> *For they are LIFE unto those that find them, and HEALTH to all their flesh.*
>
> — Proverbs 4:20-22

Two things people strive for above everything else are *life* and *health*. In His Word, God has given us a four-step recipe for attaining both of these blessings.

The first step in God's recipe for life and health is found in Proverbs 4:20: "... *attend* [listen] *to my words.* ..." God tells us that we can only find life and health *through His Word.*

The Bible says Jesus is the living Word of God.

JOHN 1:1-3,14
1   In the beginning was the Word, and the Word was with God, and THE WORD WAS GOD.
2   The same was in the beginning with God.
3   All things were made by HIM; and without HIM was not any thing made that was made. ...
14 And THE WORD was MADE FLESH, and dwelt among us. ...

The *written* Word is given to reveal the *living*

Word — the Lord Jesus Christ — to us.

In John 10:10, Jesus said, *". . . I am come that they might have life, and that they might have it more abundantly."* The reason Jesus, the living Word, came was so that man might have *life.*

Jesus didn't come to give mankind new rules to use to climb a heavenly stairway to the glory world. Jesus didn't come to give man a new code of conduct. He didn't come to bring man a system of teaching that would enable him to become God-like. Jesus came to bring *life.* He came so we might have life *more abundantly.*

The Bible says we need to attend to God's Word. God's Word doesn't just mean the words Jesus actually spoke as recorded in the Gospels! Yes, we need to listen to what Jesus Himself said. But the entire New Testament, particularly the epistles, also unveils Jesus to us. We need to attend to *all* of God's Word.

No one could study the four Gospels alone and be a successful Christian. The four Gospels are a history of the life of Jesus: His works, His sayings, and His deeds. In the Gospels we see Jesus dying, but if we don't go further than the Gospels, we won't know *why* He died.

Even after Jesus was crucified and raised from the dead, His disciples didn't understand why He died. They asked Him, *". . . Lord, wilt thou at this time restore again the kingdom to Israel?"* (Acts 1:6). They were still looking for an earthly kingdom.

It is only in the epistles where we learn what this living Word, Jesus Christ, wrought for us in His death, burial, and resurrection. For instance, Second Corinthians 5:21 tells us that we were made righteous in Christ: *"For he hath made him to be sin for us, who knew no sin; that WE MIGHT BE MADE THE RIGHTEOUS-NESS OF GOD in him."*

And it's in the epistles where we learn that Jesus redeemed us from the curse of the Law and made us partakers of the blessings of the Abrahamic covenant.

> **GALATIANS 3:13,14**
> **13 CHRIST HATH REDEEMED US FROM THE CURSE OF THE LAW, being made a curse for us: for it is written, Cursed is every one that hangeth on a tree:**
> **14 That the BLESSING OF ABRAHAM MIGHT COME ON THE GENTILES through Jesus Christ. . . .**

It's also in the epistles where we read, *"For the wages of sin is death; but THE GIFT OF GOD IS ETERNAL LIFE through Jesus Christ our Lord"* (Rom. 6:23). These are just a few of the many references in the epistles that tell us what belongs to us through Jesus Christ. We need to attend or listen to these truths in God's Word, for they will bring us life and health in every area of our lives.

The second step in God's recipe for life and health is also found in Proverbs 4:20: *". . . INCLINE THINE EAR unto my sayings. . . ."* If you want to walk in the fullness of life and health, give God's Word your undivided attention. Put everything away from your mind that contradicts what God's Word says. Accept God's

Word and act upon what it says.

We are to open our ears to God's sayings and close our ears to everything else. We are to listen to what *God* has to say. By believing the Word and accepting it, His Word will work for us.

While praying to the Father, Jesus said, ". . . *thy word is truth*" (John 17:17). Jesus also said, "*And ye shall know the truth, and the truth shall make you free*" (John 8:32). No man will ever know life, freedom, and truth without giving his full attention to knowing God's Word.

Knowing God's Word has a twofold application because Jesus *is* the living Word of God. You begin to know Jesus personally by accepting Him as your Savior. But you will never know Jesus, the living Word, in His fullness without knowing the written Word of God.

Too many people try to understand God by feelings. Smith Wigglesworth said, "I cannot understand God by feelings. I cannot understand the Lord Jesus Christ by feelings. I understand God, and I understand Jesus through the Word of God. God is everything the Word says He is. Get acquainted with God through the Word. Get acquainted with the Lord Jesus Christ through the Word."

The third step in God's recipe for life and health is found in Proverbs 4:21. It says, "*Let them* [my words] *NOT DEPART FROM THINE EYES. . . .*" We are to *look* as well as to *listen* to God's Word. The Bible says to keep our vision fixed on Jesus (Heb. 12:2). How do you do that? Continue to feed upon the written Word, and

Jesus, the living Word, will become more real to you every day.

We should also keep our vision fixed on Jesus when it comes to the healing of our bodies. I learned the importance of doing this one night a number of years ago, when I was troubled with alarming physical symptoms. I knelt by my bedside to pray, and I claimed the promises of God regarding healing. Then I got into bed. But the symptoms only grew worse.

I continued to praise God for my healing and finally managed to fall asleep. But almost immediately I was awakened by the same symptoms. Finally, I said, "Lord, I don't know how much longer I can take this."

I continued to praise the Lord and soon fell asleep again. However, I was awakened the second time. Then in my spirit I heard the words, "Consider not." I began to rejoice because I knew that passage of Scripture in Romans 4 the Holy Spirit was referring to. You see, the Holy Spirit will always lead and guide us in line with the Word.

Romans 4:19-21 says that Abraham ". . . *CONSIDERED NOT his own body now dead, . . . neither yet the deadness of Sarah's womb . . . but was strong in faith, giving glory to God; And being fully persuaded that, what he* [God] *had promised, he was able also to perform.*"

Abraham had God's promise that Isaac would be born. In fact, God didn't say He *was going* to do it. He said, "I *have made* thee the father of many nations" (Gen. 17:5). That's past tense.

God sees the future better than we see the past. He speaks as if it is already done, because in His sight it *is* done.

Abraham's physical senses told him it was impossible to father a child at his old age (he was about a hundred years old). Yet he ". . . *considered not his own body . . .*" and remained strong in his faith in God and what God had promised him.

In my own case, as the alarming symptoms persisted that night, my physical senses told me I was getting no better fast! But after I heard the Holy Spirit's words, "Consider not," I didn't pay attention to my body anymore. Instead, I just rejoiced in the promises of God.

However, the symptoms and the pain persisted. I finally said, "Lord, I'm not considering my body. I'm keeping my mind off the pain as much as I can, and I'm praising You for my healing. But it's a little difficult, and I don't seem to be making much progress."

Then the Holy Spirit spoke again to my spirit and said, "Consider *Him.*" Once again, I knew which scripture the Holy Spirit was referring to: *"Wherefore, holy brethren, partakers of the heavenly calling, CONSIDER the Apostle and High Priest of our profession, CHRIST JESUS"* (Heb. 3:1).

I saw it! I had been obeying the scripture that said "Consider not," but I hadn't been considering *Jesus!*

Some people think, *If I close my eyes, the problem will go away.* But at the same time the Bible tells us *not* to consider the things that are against us, it tells us what we should consider — Jesus Christ.

So I began to consider Jesus. I fixed my vision on Him instead of on the symptoms in my body. I began to consider the Word that said, *". . . Himself took our infirmities, and bare our sicknesses"* (Matt. 8:17). I began to consider Isaiah 53:4 as it is found in Dr. Isaac Leeser's literal Hebrew translation: *". . . our diseases did he bear himself, and our pains he carried: while we indeed esteemed him stricken, smitten of God, and afflicted."*

I began to meditate on the fact that Jesus bore my sickness and my pains. Soon I fell into a deep sleep. I rested well and awoke the next morning healed.

Many would agree that God is interested in our spiritual life and health. But I am so glad our text says God's words are *". . . life unto those that find them, and health to all their FLESH"* (Prov. 4:22). God is interested in our *physical* health, as well as our *spiritual* health.

Man still continues the age-old search to find man-made remedies to heal sickness and disease. Millions and millions of dollars are spent each year and thousands of lives are dedicated to find the cure for certain diseases that take their toll on humanity.

But God gave us the remedy for every sickness and disease when He sent His Son, Jesus, into this world. Jesus was a revelation of the Father's will, the living Word of God to mankind (John 1:1).

The writer of Hebrews said, *"God, who at sundry times and in divers manners spake in time past unto the fathers by the prophets, Hath in these last days SPOKEN UNTO US BY HIS SON . . ."* (Heb. 1:1,2). Jesus is God speaking to us. If you want to hear God, listen to Jesus!

For instance, one day Jesus approached a lonely leper, who cried, "... *Lord, if thou wilt, thou canst make me clean*" (Matt. 8:2).

Jesus said, "... *I will; be thou clean ...*" (Matt. 8:3). In other words, Jesus was saying, "I *am* willing." And that leper was healed. That statement proclaims God's will concerning healing forever! That is God speaking today! God is *always* willing to heal!

Unfortunately, many have not been taught that God wants to heal us, or that the Word promises healing through the redemptive work of Christ. I was never taught that as I was growing up. So as a teenage boy as I lay dying on the bed of sickness, I didn't understand that God wanted to heal me.

I had been given up to die by the best doctors in the land. But something on the inside told me I would find my answer in the Bible, so I read the Bible by day and slept with it by night. I found out that not only did God say His words are life unto those who find them, but He also said they are *health* to all their *flesh* (Prov. 4:22).

My mind couldn't understand that, but my heart believed it. And, thank God, as I learned how to listen to the Holy Spirit and believe God's Word, my body did become healthy. I was and am healed.

If we follow the Holy Spirit, He will always lead us in line with the Word of God. And the Word is Spirit-anointed and Spirit-inspired (2 Tim. 3:16). So the Spirit and the Word will always agree (John 16:13; 1 John 5:6,7).

The fourth step in God's recipe for life and health is also found in Proverbs 4:21: *". . . keep them* [My words] *in the midst of thine HEART."* Walking in life and health always starts in your heart or spirit. For instance, I knew in my *heart* that I was healed before my *body* responded to that knowledge.

Also, a person knows in his heart he is saved even before there is any outward evidence of salvation. Why? Because he has received by faith God's promise of salvation and believed it in his heart. That's what causes the outward evidence of salvation to be manifested. It is first by believing the Word in one's *heart*.

In regard to salvation, many have put "the cart before the horse," as the saying goes. They want to have some kind of feeling *first* before they believe they have received. They want some kind of external evidence so they can know they are saved. But salvation starts on the inside — by *believing* in the spirit or heart.

As a new Christian believes the Word and keeps it in his heart, it causes the life of God to spring up in him. The more he feeds upon the Word, the more he'll be able to walk in the light of the Word that is in him.

The same principle is true in regard to physical healing. For instance, when I received the revelation of Mark 11:23,24 in my heart when I lay sick and dying, and I stood in faith for my healing, I knew in my innermost being that I was healed. I praised God for my healing even when my heart still didn't beat right and my body was still partially paralyzed. I kept that Word in the midst of my heart.

It's a mistake to start looking at your body to see if you are healed. The Bible says, *"God is a Spirit . . ."* (John 4:24), and He heals you through your spirit. In other words, healing begins in your spirit and then is manifested in your body.

Jesus said, *". . . the words that I speak unto you, they are spirit, and they are life"* (John 6:63). The Word of God is a God-breathed, God-inspired, and God-indwelt message. Always keep these God-inspired words in the midst of your heart.

You have the living Word, Jesus Christ, dwelling within you by the Holy Spirit. Paul said, *". . . Christ IN you, the hope of glory"* (Col. 1:27). The more you feed upon the written Word, the more real the living Word becomes in you, and the more you learn how to appropriate what He is in you.

So if you want to walk in the light of life and find health for your body, continually listen to God's Word. Give God's Word your undivided attention. Fix your vision on Jesus, the living Word. Keep God's Word in the midst of your heart. Why are these four steps so important? Because God's words "are *life* unto all who find them and *health* to all their flesh"!

Chapter 8
Fellowship With the Holy Spirit

However, I am telling you nothing but the truth when I say, it is profitable — good, expedient, advantageous — for you that I go away. Because if I do not go away, the Comforter (Counselor, Helper, Advocate, Intercessor, Strengthener, Standby) will not come to you — into close fellowship with you. But if I go away, I will send Him to you — to be in close fellowship with you.
— John 16:7 *(Amp.)*

The *Amplified* translation of John 16:7 gives us the sevenfold meaning of the Greek word translated "Comforter" in the *King James Version*: Comforter, Counselor, Helper, Advocate, Intercessor, Strengthener, or Standby. Let us look briefly at each meaning.

First, the Holy Spirit is our *Helper*. Often we look to the wrong place for help. How many of us look on the inside for help? How many of us depend on Him who is dwelling within us to help us? Sometimes we run all over the country looking for some minister to help us instead of turning to the Greater One on the inside.

Yes, God put ministers in the Church to teach and help people. But will they always be there in your time of need? No! But if you are born again, the Holy Spirit is always in you as a *Comforter* to help and comfort you in any need. If you depend upon Him to comfort you, He will do it. You'll have comfort from within. People won't be able to understand how you can be so composed and at peace in times of trouble. But you'll know why. Thank God, the Comforter lives within you!

Second, the Holy Spirit is your *Counselor*. He'll counsel with you. And the Scriptures say He will lead you into all truth (John 16:13).

Third, He's your *Advocate*. The word "advocate" means *lawyer* or *one who pleads your cause*. As an advocate, He'll help you. He knows how to plead your case.

Fourth, the Holy Spirit is your *Intercessor*. This has to do with your prayer life. Romans 8:26 says, *"Likewise the Spirit also helpeth our infirmities: for we know not what we should pray for as we ought: but the Spirit itself* [Himself] *maketh intercession for us with groanings which cannot be uttered."*

Paul is talking about what the Holy Spirit will do to help believers in prayer as He dwells inside them. Notice Paul, writing to the Romans, is talking to people who are not only born of the Spirit, but who are also filled with the Spirit.

Fifth, the *Amplified* translation of John 14:16 goes on to say that the Holy Spirit is your *Strengthener*. Have you ever thought about looking on the inside for strength? Or are you waiting for God to send something down from Heaven on you to strengthen you? Are you singing, "Come by here, Lord! Come by here!" when the Holy Spirit is already dwelling within you to give you strength?

Sixth, the Holy Spirit is your *Standby.* He's just standing by waiting for you to ask for His help. Maybe the reason He hasn't done anything for you is that you haven't asked Him. He is standing by to help you any time you need Him.

Often instead of trusting and depending on the Holy Spirit, we try to figure out a solution to our problems in the flesh. We often pray primarily out of our heads, which are sometimes confused, perplexed, and worried. We worry before we pray, while we pray, and after we pray. When we pray like that, our praying doesn't amount to a hill of beans.

Instead of letting the Holy Spirit help us and comfort us, too often we depend on our flesh and our own mental capacities to find answers to our needs. At times I've done that. When I was a young Christian, sometimes I prayed for hours about a problem when I knew what the Word said about it all the time. I just wore myself out for nothing. It was like a dark cloud hanging over my head, when my answer was in the Word all the time.

Has that ever happened to you? Have you ever been so mentally upset and concerned about things that have happened that you felt like someone had mentally beaten you? When that happens, you're trying to figure out the solution in your mind. Your mind is confused, and you're just wearing yourself out mentally.

But the Holy Spirit is not in your head. He's in your heart — in your spirit. Your body is a temple of the Holy Ghost because your body is a temple of your *own* spirit. The Holy Spirit dwells in your spirit.

It's so wonderful in the midst of perplexity to have the Holy Spirit right there in your spirit standing by you. You can actually find rest in the midst of the battle with Him on the inside of you. You can come to the place where you just laugh out loud when nothing seems to be going right. When you wake up in the night, instead of worrying, you can just start laughing. You can laugh because you have inside information.

Years ago, a woman came to our home early one morning who needed to learn how to call upon the Holy Spirit inside of her. Sometime before she had been healed of sugar diabetes and from a tumor in her body. I had sent a prayer cloth to her through her sister, who was a member of a church I had pastored.

The woman came to our parsonage for prayer. To make a long story short, she said she was sick again, but that if she could get back to God, she didn't care if she lived or died. When she said that, I thought she must have committed some awful sin.

I told her God would forgive her of whatever she had done wrong. She looked at me and said she hadn't done anything wrong. I asked her what made her think she had lost the victory. She said that she didn't *feel* like she had the victory. Actually, there was nothing wrong with this woman except that she was walking by feelings and not by faith.

I told her that if I always went by my feelings, I would sometimes have to ask the congregation to pray for me when I got up to preach because I don't always *feel* like a Christian. Many times I don't *feel* a thing. Thank God our salvation isn't based on feelings; it's based on the Word of God!

The woman looked at me in astonishment and said, "You mean, preachers feel that way sometimes too?"

I told her, "Preachers are human just like you are."

She asked me, "What do you do when you feel spiritually dry?"

I told her, "Just sit there and watch what I do."

Then I shut my eyes, lifted my hands, and said, "Heavenly Father, I want to thank You today because I am your child. I've been born again and I'm a child of God. Second Corinthians 5:17 says that I'm a new creature. I'm your very own child and You are my very own Father, for I'm born of God.

"I want to thank You because You're living with me and in me. I want to thank You for the gift of the Holy Ghost. I want to thank You because He is in me. First John 2:27 says that the anointing abides in me. That anointing is in me and I want to thank You for it."

About that time way down on the inside of me I felt that fire and that thrill of the Presence of the Greater One dwelling on the inside of me. I felt something start to bubble. I had been stirring up the fire of the Holy Spirit in my spirit. I began to laugh and talk in tongues.

The woman said, "Your very expression changed and lit up as you were speaking!"

I told her, "I can understand that. I began to feel differently as I talked to the Lord."

She asked, "Can I do that?"

"Certainly you can," I answered.

So the woman did the same thing that I had done, and then she began to laugh and talk in tongues. She exclaimed, "I've had that joy inside me all the time! I just didn't know it!"

That's the trouble with a lot of folks. They have the victory inside of them and don't even know it. They've been going by their feelings and struggling in the flesh with their problem, when all they need to do is stir up the anointing within them.

You always have the anointing — the Holy Spirit — within you to help you pray and to help you in every area of life (1 John 2:20). The Bible says He *abides* in you (1 John 2:27). Someone still might say, "But I don't feel Him." The Holy Spirit is in you just as much when you *don't* feel His Presence as He is when you *do* feel His Presence. If He came and then went, He wouldn't be *abiding* within you.

First, you have to believe the Bible because it says you do have Him abiding within. Second, you have to do what Paul told Timothy: *"Wherefore I put thee in remembrance that thou STIR UP THE GIFT OF GOD, which is in thee by the putting on of my hands"* (2 Tim. 1:6). What was Paul talking about when he said "stir up the gift of God that is within you"? He was talking about the gift of the Holy Ghost.

You see, in Second Timothy 1:6, Paul talks about the gift of God being given through the laying on of hands. Then in the next verse he says God has *given* us a *spirit*

of power, love, and a sound mind — the Holy Spirit (2 Tim. 1:7).

Combine these verses with First Corinthians 6:19, which tells us our bodies are the temple of the Holy Ghost who is *in* us. It seems quite obvious to me that the gift of God Paul is talking about in Second Timothy 1:6 is the Holy Ghost.

In First John 2:27 when John talked about the anointing abiding within the believer, he was referring to the Holy Spirit. And Jesus talked about the Holy Spirit, calling Him the Comforter, Counselor, Helper, Advocate, Intercessor, Strengthener, and Standby (John 16:7 *Amp.*).

Fire is a type of the Holy Ghost (Luke 3:16; Acts 2:3,4). Stir up the fire that is within you. You can stir up the anointing within you. Paul wrote to the Church at Rome and said, "Be fervent in spirit" (Rom. 12:11). *Moffatt's* translation says, "Maintain the spiritual glow."

God gave you the fire and the anointing of the Holy Spirit within. But it's up to you to do something about it. It's up to you to "maintain the glow." You need to stir up the embers and the inner fire of the Holy Spirit. It's up to *you* to stir Him up!

The *Amplified* translation of Romans 12:11 says, "Never lag in zeal and in earnest endeavor; be aglow and burning with the Spirit, serving the Lord." The Spirit is fire. Be aglow and afire with the Spirit!

How does all this apply to our prayer life? It is through praying in the Spirit that we stir up our inner fire. We must maintain the glow in our prayer life. We don't need to pray that God will give us the Holy Ghost. He is already inside of us to be our Comforter, Counselor, Helper, Advocate, Intercessor, Strengthener, and Standby! The New Testament says the Holy Spirit abides in us (John 14:17,23). We just need to recognize that fact and stir up the Gift of God within!

Chapter 9
Following the Inward Witness

> *For as many as are led by the Spirit of God,*
> *they are the sons of God. . . .*
> *The Spirit itself [Himself] beareth witness*
> *with our spirit, that we are the children of God.*
> — Romans 8:14,16

> *The spirit of man is the candle of the Lord,*
> *searching all the inward parts of the belly.*
> — Proverbs 20:27

Many times Christians try to receive guidance other than how the Bible says we are to receive. For example, nowhere in the Bible does it say God guides us through our *souls*. People sometimes use the words "spirit" and "soul" interchangeably. But they are not interchangeable, and people who don't understand that can become hopelessly confused.

We know from the Word that man's soul and spirit do not refer to the same thing because the Bible differentiates between them. It says, *". . . the word of God is quick, and powerful, and sharper than any twoedged sword, piercing even to the DIVIDING ASUNDER of SOUL and SPIRIT . . ."* (Heb. 4:12).

Paul writing to the church at Thessalonica also made a distinction between the three parts of man's being: ". . . *I pray God your whole SPIRIT and SOUL and BODY be preserved blameless unto the coming of our Lord Jesus Christ*" (1 Thess. 5:23).

Actually, the Word of God teaches that you *are* a spirit, you *have* a soul, and you *live* in a body.

If you're born again, the Holy Spirit is abiding in your spirit.

> **JOHN 14:16,17**
> **16 And I will pray the Father, and he shall give you another Comforter, that he may abide with you for ever;**
> **17 Even the Spirit of truth; whom the world cannot receive, because it seeth him not, neither knoweth him: but ye know him; for he dwelleth with you, and shall be in you.**

Since God dwells *in* you — in your heart or spirit — that is where He is going to speak to you. He does not communicate directly with your mind, because He's not in your mind; He's in your spirit. The margin of Proverbs 20:27 reads, "The spirit of man is the *lamp* of the Lord. . . ." That means God will guide or enlighten us through our *spirits*.

You see, you are a spirit being, and you contact the *spiritual* realm with your spirit. You contact the *mental* realm with your intellect. And you contact the *physical* realm with your body.

It is your spirit that becomes a new creation in Christ when you are born again.

> **2 CORINTHIANS 5:17**
> **17 Therefore if any man be in Christ, HE IS A NEW**

CREATURE: **old things are passed away** [in his
spirit]; **behold, all things are become new.**

When we are born again, we still have the same
body we had before. The outward man doesn't change.
But the spirit man *on the inside* has become a new man
in Christ. And because God guides us through our
spirit, it's important to allow that inward man to dominate our lives.

How does God guide us? Romans 8:14,16 tells us
that we are to be led *by the Holy Spirit* as He *bears witness* with our spirit. The number one way God guides
all of His children is by the *inward witness*.

Let me explain what I mean by the "inward witness." Suppose you pray about going in a certain direction in your life, and you get a *check* or a *red light* in
your spirit. Or to say it another way, on the inside of
you there is something that tells you *no* or *stop*. On the
inside — in your heart — you just don't feel good about
going in the direction you're praying about.

That check in your spirit is the Holy Spirit telling
you *not* to go in that direction, no matter how good circumstances look on the outside. On the other hand, if
you pray about a matter and you get a *go-ahead signal*
or a *velvety-like* feeling in your heart, that's the witness
of the Holy Spirit to proceed.

When Jesus appeared to me in a vision in February
1959, He walked into my room, sat down beside me, and
talked to me for an hour and a half. Most of that time He
talked to me about the prophet's ministry, but He also

talked to me about how to be led by the Spirit of God.

Jesus mentioned the fact that although the prophet's ministry under the New Covenant is similar to the prophet's ministry under the Old Covenant, New Testament prophets don't have the same status as Old Testament prophets. Under the Old Covenant, those we would call laymen didn't have the Holy Ghost, so they had to go to the prophet for direction.

Jesus said to me in that vision, "Under the New Covenant, it is unscriptural to go to a prophet for direction, because every Christian has the Spirit of God *within* to lead and guide him."

Sometimes a prophet may *confirm* something you already have in your spirit, but he is never to give you guidance apart from the leading you've already received from the Lord.

Then in this vision Jesus talked to me about two different churches where I had been invited to hold meetings. He specifically told me to go to one of them and not to go to the other one. He said, "Now you see Me sitting here talking to you about which church to go to. But I'm not going to lead you this way again. I'm going to lead you just like I do all of My children — by the inward witness."

A lot of times people think, *Oh, Brother Hagin has it made, standing in the office of the prophet. God talks to him.* But a prophet has to seek God and pray through in order to get guidance for his life just like anyone else does. God doesn't have any favorite children.

The Lord said to me, "Many of My children miss it

because they are waiting for the spectacular, and they are missing the supernatural." You see, the inward witness of the Holy Spirit is *supernatural.* The inward witness is God communicating supernaturally with our spirits.

So first, God leads His children by the *inward witness.* Second, He leads us by the *inward voice.* With the inward voice, our own spirit speaks to us what it picks up from the Holy Ghost. God also can lead us by the more *authoritative Voice* of the Holy Spirit. When the Holy Ghost within us speaks, it can almost seem to be an audible Voice.

In our text we read that *"The Spirit itself* [Himself] *BEARETH WITNESS with our spirit . . ."* (Rom. 8:16). Many Christians think Paul is talking here about some kind of *physical* witness or evidence. But that's not what he's talking about at all. Paul doesn't say, "The Spirit Himself bears witness with our physical senses or our *bodies.*" No, he says the Holy Spirit bears witness with our *spirits.*

You can't base your Christian walk on your physical senses or your feelings. Many times your feelings will tell you that you're not even saved!

Write this down and don't forget it: *Feeling* is the voice of the body. *Reason* is the voice of your soul or mind. And *conscience* is the voice of your spirit.

Your inward man has a voice; it is your conscience! Is your conscience a safe guide? It is if your spirit has been born again and your mind renewed by the Word of God.

Remember that in the new birth, your spirit became

new. Your conscience is the voice of that new man. If your spirit is a new creation with the life and nature of God, and your mind has been renewed by God's Word, then your conscience is a safe guide.

However, a person who has never been born again could not follow the voice of his spirit. His spirit is unregenerate; therefore, his conscience could permit him to sin. But when a person has the life and nature of God in him, his conscience is pricked and his heart is grieved if he sins.

If you are being led by your feelings or by your physical senses instead of by your conscience, you are heading for trouble. You contact this world where Satan is god with your physical senses. If your mind or body is dominating you, Satan can find entrance into your life and begin to control you through your feelings or senses.

You can't walk by faith if you're led by your feelings. It makes no difference whether or not you *feel* like something is so, or whether or not you *feel* like God heard you when you prayed. If the Word of God says it, then it's true!

Sometimes I hear people say, "I believe God heard my prayer. I just *feel* like He did." I never say that. Instead I say, "God heard my prayer because His Word said He did!"

God said, *"Call unto me, AND I WILL ANSWER THEE, and shew thee great and mighty things, which thou knowest not"* (Jer. 33:3). If God's Word says He hears and answers prayer, then He does!

Base your faith on the Word, not on your feelings or

senses. Feelings, the voice of your body, may tell you a
lot of things that are contrary to God's Word. But the
Holy Spirit will communicate to you through your
spirit, and it will always be in line with the Word.

> **JOHN 16:13**
> **13 Howbeit when he, THE SPIRIT OF TRUTH**
> [that is, the Holy Spirit], **is come, he will GUIDE YOU**
> **INTO ALL TRUTH: for he shall not speak of him-**
> **self; but whatsoever he shall hear, that shall he**
> **speak: and he will shew you things to come.**

Jesus said the Holy Spirit will show you things to
come. How will He do that? By bearing witness with your
spirit! The Holy Spirit dwells in your spirit, endeavoring
to lead and guide you in all the affairs of life.

Now let's look at a biblical illustration of how this
inward witness operates.

> **ACTS 27:9,10**
> **9 Now when much time was spent, and when**
> **sailing was now dangerous, because the fast was**
> **now already past, Paul admonished them,**
> **10 And said unto them, Sirs, I PERCEIVE that this**
> **voyage will be with hurt and much damage, not**
> **only of the lading and ship, but also of our lives.**

Notice Paul didn't say, "The Lord told me." He didn't
say the Spirit of God said anything to him, although at
other times in the Bible the Holy Spirit did speak to
Paul. Paul said, "I *perceive*."

Who is the real "I" that Paul is referring to? The
real "I" is the inward man or the spirit man on the

inside. Paul didn't perceive this mentally. He didn't perceive it physically through his senses. But in his spirit he had *an inward witness* that ". . . *this voyage will be with hurt and much damage. . . .*" The Holy Spirit was showing him things to come (John 16:13).

Every Christian ought to have a certain amount of that kind of spiritual perception. I'm not talking about a manifestation of a gift of the Spirit here, such as the word of wisdom or the word of knowledge. I know when the word of knowledge is operating, because it has operated through me more than any other gift of the Spirit. But I also recognize that inward witness or perception of the Holy Spirit in my own spirit.

I know a Full Gospel pastor who years ago was in a serious automobile accident. Several cars were involved and his wife was almost killed. After hearing me teach about being led by the Holy Spirit, he told me, "On the day of the accident as my wife and I were preparing to travel, something on the inside of me said, 'Wait here ten minutes.'

"It was just an inward perception, and I had a sense that something bad was about to happen. However, instead of waiting ten minutes, I thought, *We've already prayed and confessed the Word concerning protection, so nothing is going to happen to us.*"

You might ask, "If that pastor and his wife prayed and believed God, why did the accident happen?" Well, God *did* answer their prayer! He was trying to protect them by warning them to wait until the danger had passed.

This is where "faith" people miss it: They haven't understood the ministry of the Holy Ghost. They haven't understood how to follow the inward witness.

You see, you can make all the faith confessions you want to, but if the Holy Ghost has already told you to do something, you'd better obey Him. If you don't, you're in disobedience, and your faith confessions won't do a bit of good.

A minister once told me that he and his family were sitting in a restaurant one evening ready to place their order, when suddenly the minister said to his wife, "We have to go home."

This minister didn't have a word from God. He just *perceived* something was wrong at home. (If it had been a word of knowledge, he would have known exactly what the problem was.) So he and his family left the restaurant and drove home. Just as they drove into the driveway, the hot water heater blew up in their garage!

Since they were there when it happened, they contacted the fire department immediately and the fire was put out before it did much damage. But what if the minister hadn't obeyed that inward witness? The whole house could have burned to the ground.

We need to make sure we aren't trying to tell God *how* to lead us. Too many times when God is trying to lead believers through the inward witness, they don't take the time to listen. Many times they are hoping God will lead them in a more spectacular way, such as through a vision, an audible voice, or an angelic visitation.

Those more spectacular kinds of guidance may occur or they may not. These things happen as the Spirit wills. But God never promised us that we would be led by visions, voices, or angelic visitations. He did, however, promise to lead us by the inward witness (Rom. 8:14,16).

The inward witness often takes waiting before God to discern what He's saying. The problem with a lot of Christians is they don't want to take the time to seek God until they know what God's will is concerning a matter. They just don't want to take the responsibility of finding God's will for their lives.

Sometimes there's a price to pay in order to receive God's guidance for your life. Often it takes waiting before God in prayer and in the Word long enough to get all of your physical senses under control, because your body is always clamoring for attention. And sometimes it means waiting long enough to get your mind quiet, because your mind can be just as noisy as your body.

But once you get your body under control and your mind quiet, you can begin to understand what God is saying to you. *You can understand what God is saying every time, if you'll take the time to wait before Him.*

It may take longer for some people than for others to get their flesh under subjection to their spirit so they can hear God, because they've allowed their flesh to dominate them for so long. But once they get their mind and their physical senses under control, they'll be able to hear what God is saying to their *spirit*.

A key principle to following the inward witness I

learned early in life was to *develop and train my spirit.*
Throughout my Christian walk I have endeavored to do
that as diligently as I could.

How do you train your spirit? Number one, feed on
God's Word. Jesus said, ". . . *Man shall not live by bread
alone, but by every word that proceedeth out of the
mouth of God*" (Matt. 4:4).

Number two, make sure you walk in love. When I
was still a teenager, I made a quality decision that I
was always going to walk in love, regardless of whether
or not anyone else did.

Number three, pray much in other tongues. I know
from experience that praying in other tongues is one of
the best ways to develop your spirit man.

> **1 CORINTHIANS 14:14**
> **14 For if I pray in an unknown tongue, MY SPIRIT
> PRAYETH. . . .**

Praying in other tongues helps your mind become
quiet. You might have problems getting your mind quiet
at first, but keep on until you succeed. As you pray in
tongues, don't let your mind wander off and think
whatever it wants. Set your mind on Jesus. Just think
about Him, and your mind will eventually become
quiet.

Once your mind is quiet, you will become more conscious of your spirit, because you're praying out of your
spirit. You see, your mind doesn't even have to think,
because tongues come out of your spirit, not your head!

When you pray out of your heart or spirit, you

become more conscious of your own spirit and of spiritual things. Supernaturally you're in direct contact with God, the Father of spirits (Heb. 12:9).

If you'll develop your spirit man, after a while you'll know on the inside what to do in every situation in life. You'll have a "yes" or a "no" in your spirit, and you'll know just what you should do even in the minor incidents of life.

Too many of us spend most of our lives living in the mental and the physical realms. Many times we've developed our intellects at the expense of developing our hearts. Our intellects take the throne in our lives, and our spirits, which *should* guide us, are kept locked away in prison and are not permitted to function. But whether or not we listen to our spirits, the Holy Spirit through the inward witness is always seeking to give guidance to our minds.

Let's learn to be sensitive to the Holy Ghost! Let's get acquainted with the One who lives *in* us. I think many Christians have never really gotten acquainted with Him. They only know Him in a general or a vague sense, as if He is some sort of far-off *something*.

But the Bible says the Holy Spirit is in you as your Comforter, Counselor, Helper, Intercessor, Advocate, Strengthener, and Standby (John 14:26 *Amp.*). And if you will learn to let your spirit dominate your mind and flesh, then ". . . *he will guide you into all truth . . . and he will shew you things to come*" (John 16:13).

You are the temple of the living God (1 Cor. 3:16)! Never take that truth for granted. Train your spirit

man to listen to the Holy Spirit who dwells inside you.
Renew your mind with the Word of God and refuse to
allow your flesh to dominate you. As you do, you will
learn to follow the inward witness!

Chapter 10
Accountable to God's Call

For the gifts and calling of God are without
repentance.

— Romans 11:29

Are you a child of God? If you have been born again, then you are called of God. You have a call upon your life to fulfill the specific plan and purpose which God has ordained for *you* (Eph. 2:10). Even before you became a child of God, that call was there, for God chose you before the foundation of the world (Eph. 1:4).

You cannot escape the call of God. The Bible says the gifts and calling of God are without repentance (Rom. 11:29). That means God will never change His mind about the gifts and the call He has given you. The call of God on your life will be with you as long as you live. And one day you will stand before the Judgment Seat of Christ to give an account of that call (Rom. 14:10-12; 2 Cor. 5:10).

When you stand before Jesus, if you haven't done what He has told you to do, you won't be able to use the excuse, "Lord, I just *couldn't* fulfill my call." Notice Romans 11:29 says, ". . . *the GIFTS and calling of God are without repentance.*" So whatever God calls you to do, He will also gift you to be able to accomplish. In other words, He will furnish you with the spiritual endowment or equipment to fulfill your call. If you will simply be faithful, God will bless you and make you a success in what He has called you to do.

For example, the Apostle Paul was faithful to the call of God upon his life to the very end. From the moment of Paul's conversion on the road to Damascus to the day of his death, Paul endeavored to fulfill God's will in his life and ministry.

Acts 9 relates Paul's conversion on the road to Damascus. Paul, called Saul of Tarsus at that time, was persecuting Christians in the mistaken belief that he was fulfilling the will of God. But on the Damascus road, Jesus stopped Saul in his tracks by speaking to him in a heavenly vision.

> **ACTS 9:3-5**
> **3** . . . **suddenly there shined round about him** [Saul] **a light from heaven:**
> **4** **And he fell to earth, and heard a voice saying unto him, SAUL, SAUL, WHY PERSECUTEST THOU ME?**
> **5** **And he said, Who art thou, Lord? And the Lord said, I AM JESUS WHOM THOU PERSECUTEST....**

Many years later, Paul recounted the story of the Damascus road vision as he stood before King Agrippa (Acts 26:13-19). In this account of the vision, Paul related what Jesus had said about Paul's call, including the fact that Paul was sent to the Gentiles (Acts 26:16-18). Paul also made another important statement about the call God had placed upon his life: *"Whereupon, O king Agrippa, I WAS NOT DISOBEDIENT UNTO THE*

HEAVENLY VISION" (Acts 26:19). Or we could read it this way: "I was obedient to the heavenly call." That should also be *our* testimony before men!

As we look at Paul's life in the Book of Acts, we can see how he obeyed his call as God led him through different stages of ministry. You see, God never *removes* the call He has placed on a person's life, but He may *add* something to that call. He may start a person in one area of ministry. Then after a period of time, if the person proves faithful to what God has told him to do, God may promote that person to another area of ministry.

For instance, we can see from Acts 13 that earlier in Paul's and Barnabus' ministries, they each stood in the offices of either *prophet* or *teacher* or both.

ACTS 13:1,2
1 Now there were in the church that was at Antioch certain PROPHETS and TEACHERS; as BARNABUS, and Simeon that was called Niger, and Lucius of Cyrene, and Manaen, . . . and SAUL.
2 As they ministered to the Lord, and fasted, the Holy Ghost said, Separate me BARNABUS and SAUL for the WORK whereunto I HAVE CALLED THEM.

It was at this time that Paul and Barnabus were sent forth by the Holy Ghost to proclaim the gospel to the Gentiles (Acts 13:4). It was also at this time that God added to each of their calls and moved them both into a new stage of ministry, because in Acts 14:14, Paul and Barnabus were called *apostles*. These two men didn't stand in the office of apostle to begin with in their ministries. God promoted both of them after they had been in the ministry for some time.

Why didn't God place Paul and Barnabus in the office of apostle earlier? Because God will prove us first before He moves us on to a new stage in His call for our lives. We need to learn to be faithful where we are right now and let God choose the timing for the next stage in our lives and ministries.

God can't use us or promote us if we are unsteady or unfaithful. That's why again and again in the epistles, Paul encourages us to be steadfast. For instance, in First Corinthians 15:58, Paul says, *"Therefore, my beloved brethren, BE YE STEDFAST, UNMOVEABLE, always abounding in the work of the Lord. . . ."*

Throughout his life, Paul obeyed the admonition to be steadfast as he remained faithful to his call. And at the end of his life, he was able to write to Timothy, *". . . I have finished my course . . ."* (2 Tim. 4:7).

Paul was faithful to fulfill God's purpose for his life. In the same way, each one of us is accountable before God to discover what God has called *us* to do by seeking Him diligently. Then each of us must be faithful to fulfill the call of God on our own lives.

Personally, I have tried to be faithful to the call of God on my life to preach ever since 1934 when I was raised off a deathbed. In my own experience, I knew all of my life even as a small child that I was called to preach.

You see, that call was on my life before I was ever born. In 1950, Jesus explained that to me when He appeared to me in a vision in Rockwall, Texas. He told

me, "I called you before you were born. I separated you
unto the ministry while you were in your mother's
womb. Satan tried to destroy your life before you were
born and many times since then, but My angels have
watched over you and cared for you until this hour."

When I was a small child and hadn't yet reached the
age of accountability, my spirit was alive to God, which
is true of every child (Rom. 7:9). That's why as a child I
knew in my spirit I was called to preach. But when I
was nine years old, I reached the age of accountability — I understood the difference between right and
wrong (reaching the age of accountability is different
for every child). At that point, I decided I would rather
be a lawyer than a preacher.

Then at fifteen years of age, I became bedfast and
eventually was born again. And just as soon as my
spirit was back in fellowship with God, the first thing I
said was, "Lord, if You will get me up from this bed, I'll
go preach."

You see, the call was still right there in my spirit.
God never removed the call during the years I wasn't in
fellowship with Him, for the gifts and calling of God are
without repentance (Rom. 11:29). God was just waiting
for me to become born again and to obey the call He had
placed on my life.

God did raise me off that bed of sickness, and I
immediately began to preach at every opportunity.
From 1934 to 1943, I was strictly a preacher. I started
out as a Southern Baptist pastor, preaching evangelistic sermons. I loved to preach. And I could preach, too,

because that's what God had anointed me to do!

But since then God has added other gifts to my call. Remember I said that although God will never take away the call on your life, He might add to it.

For instance, there was a specific time when God added the gift of teaching to my ministry. Up until then, all I ever did was preach, even when I began pastoring Pentecostal churches. I didn't like to teach.

But something happened one day in 1943 to change my attitude about teaching. I was in my home, and I had just awakened from a nap. I got up and went to the kitchen to get a drink of water.

I no more expected what happened next than I expected to be the first man to land on the moon! As I was walking back through the living room, something came down over me; it was the anointing of God. It felt just like someone had thrown a coat over me, and then it went down inside of me into my spirit. When it got down into my spirit, I knew what it was. I stopped in the middle of the living room and said, "I have a teaching gift now. I can teach!" And from then on I enjoyed teaching because God added the anointing to stand in the office of teacher to my call.

Then in the winter of 1947 and 1948, the Lord began to prepare me for a change in my ministry. I had been pastoring since 1937, and at this time I was pastoring the best church I had ever pastored. I had every reason in the world to be satisfied.

But I knew on the inside of me that something was not right. Pastoring that church was like washing my feet with my socks on; it didn't feel right. I began to wait on God in prayer.

As I waited on the Lord during that time, I found out why I had been unsatisfied in my spirit as a pastor. The Lord told me, "I never did call you to pastor to begin with. I've only *permitted* you to pastor." Then He began to talk to me further about my call and about my future ministry.

In the next few years I came to understand that the office of the prophet is my first calling. But I was in the ministry for many years before I actually stood in that office to minister.

Often God may give us some light about our call, but that doesn't mean we will step into the fullness of that call overnight. As I said, God will prove us first before moving us to different stages of our call.

So in 1949, I left the last church I ever pastored and went out into field ministry. I had been out in field ministry for about sixteen months when God revealed another part of my call. In May 1950, I heard a Voice speak to me from Heaven, saying, "I want you to go teach My people faith. You have learned faith both through My Word and by experience. Now go teach My people what I have taught you." I have endeavored to obey that heavenly Voice. Since then, I have taught on faith more than on any other subject.

Then in 1963 during a time of prayer, the Lord gave me further direction regarding my ministry. You see, as you are faithful in what God has already told you to do, He will reveal more about what He has called you to do.

First of all the Lord said to me, "Put all of your teachings on faith and healing in book form." Actually, in 1960 I had already published one book, *Redeemed From Poverty, Sickness, and Spiritual Death.* But after the Lord said that to me in 1963, I didn't want to just jump out and immediately begin to print more books. It is wise to wait before the Lord in prayer for His timing before we act on what He has told us to do.

In 1966 we printed our second book, *Right and Wrong Thinking.* From that time until the present, in the United States alone we have printed about forty-six million books in English and Spanish. That doesn't include the millions of books printed in other languages. It pays to stay faithful!

In that same time of prayer when God told me to print my messages, the Lord also said to me, "Put your messages on tape, and get on the radio and teach the Word." So we obeyed God in these instructions as well.

In 1966 we began our tape ministry. Over the years we have produced millions of tapes, sending out forty to fifty thousand tapes each month to people around the world. We had no idea our tape ministry would ever grow to be so large.

Also in 1966 we began our radio ministry. We did it because God said to do it, and it was amazing how God worked out the details. Today our radio program "Faith Seminar of the Air" is on 228 radio stations, including two shortwave stations which broadcast our program around the world.

And God continued to lead me into further changes

in my ministry. In the early 1970s, the Lord began to deal with me about starting RHEMA Bible Training Center. In 1974 we started RHEMA, graduating fifty-eight students that first year. Since then, more than 12,000 students have graduated from RHEMA — men and women who are trained to carry the gospel throughout this country and the nations of the world.

Sometimes people say, "Isn't it marvelous what Brother Hagin has done?" But I haven't done a thing in the world. Dear Lord, all I've done is just run to try and keep up with what God is doing!

The Bible says, *"Except THE LORD build the house, they labour in vain that build it . . ."* (Ps. 127:1). The Lord has built this ministry. I haven't labored at all. I have just enjoyed myself as I have done the will of God and obeyed my call.

Of course, sometimes there are hard times. But I know I am in the will of God, so I just laugh my way through them. I just lay down and go to sleep in peace right in the midst of the storm. And I say to God, "Lord, I'm doing what *You* told me to do. When You tell me to do something else, I'll do that. So I cast my cares upon You, and I'm not going to spend one minute worrying about this problem."

You see, we aren't supposed to carry a heavy load. We are only accountable for obeying the call of God on our lives, and God takes care of the rest.

I've related some details about my own experience of obeying the call of God on my life. My call is first of all to the office of the prophet and secondly to the office of the teacher. I am accountable before God to use the gifts and to fulfill the call God has given *me*.

It's important to understand that we do not all have the same gifts and callings in life. For instance, God hasn't called all of us to the pulpit ministry. But we will all be held accountable before God for *whatever* He has called *us* to do and for whatever gifts He has given to each of us in order to fulfill our call.

Have you had stirrings in your spirit regarding the call of God on your life? Perhaps you don't know altogether what that "quickening" on the inside of you means. Or perhaps you have caused that quickening of the Holy Spirit to diminish by getting caught up in the affairs of life or by trying to make your own plans. If you allow your soulish or fleshly nature to dominate you, you can temporarily shut off those stirrings in your inner man.

But when you come back to a place of waiting upon the Lord regarding His plans and purposes for you, those stirrings in you will still be there. And when you lie down at night and get quiet inside, you will still sense that quickening in your spirit, for the gifts and calling of God are without repentance (Rom. 11:29).

Don't ignore those stirrings from the Lord; seek God diligently to know what He is saying to you. You are accountable for your call! It's a sobering thought that there may be people in hell because you didn't obey God.

A time is coming when each believer will stand before the Judgment Seat of Christ to give an account for the call that God has placed upon his or her life. At that moment the only question that will really matter will be, "Were you faithful to obey the call of God on your life?"

Some who stand before Jesus on that day will have to say, "Lord, there is something I should have done, but I don't know what it was. I come before You with almost empty hands." And God's reward in Heaven for faithfulness to the call will be lost to them.

Don't be one of those who will come before Jesus with shame and regret. Seek God regarding His call on your life. Start preparing yourself early in life for whatever God has called you to do. Don't forfeit your right to God's blessings and the fullness of life by choosing to walk in the flesh or in the realm of the soul while you are on this earth. Instead, choose to obey the call of God and reap the rewards of obedience!

Be faithful to fulfill God's call, and someday you will enter into God's Presence with an abundance of fruit for the Kingdom of God. You will be able to say to Jesus, "Lord, I have obeyed the call. I have finished my course." And you will have much cause for rejoicing!

Chapter 11
Love — The Way To Make Your Faith Work

*For in Jesus Christ neither circumcision
availeth any thing, nor uncircumcision; but
FAITH WHICH WORKETH BY LOVE.*

— Galatians 5:6

*And hope maketh not ashamed; because THE
LOVE OF GOD IS SHED ABROAD IN OUR
HEARTS by the Holy Ghost which is given unto
us.*

— Romans 5:5

Both faith and love are of the heart. Notice the love
of God is shed abroad in our *hearts* by the Holy Ghost;
the love of God is *not* shed abroad in our *heads*. If you
let your head dominate you, you'll be in trouble. Also,
the Bible doesn't say the love of God is shed abroad in
our *bodies* by the Holy Ghost. No, the Bible says,
". . . *the love of God is shed abroad in our HEARTS.* . . ."

We know from Galatians 5:6 that faith works by
love. Faith is also of the heart, not of the head. Many
people get into trouble in their faith walk because they
don't understand that.

MARK 11:23
23 For verily I say unto you, That whosoever shall

116

say unto this mountain, Be thou removed, and be thou cast into the sea; and shall not doubt IN HIS HEART, but shall believe that those things which he saith shall come to pass; he shall have whatsoever he saith.

Faith will work in your heart with doubt in your head. But, you see, if people don't know that — if people are going by their heads and doubts begin to arise in their minds, they'll think they're in doubt and unbelief. But you can have faith in your heart with doubt in your head.

ROMANS 10:9,10
9 That if thou shalt confess with thy mouth the Lord Jesus, and shalt believe in thine HEART that God hath raised him from the dead, thou shalt be saved.
10 For with the HEART man BELIEVETH unto righteousness; and with the mouth confession is made unto salvation.

It's with the heart that man believes, not with the head. Faith is of the heart, and faith works by love — God's love. The God-kind of love is shed abroad in our hearts by the Holy Ghost. We didn't have that love until God gave it to us. And faith works by this kind of love.

The problem with many people is they try to substitute natural human love for divine love, or the God-kind of love, but the two are not the same. Natural human love can turn to hatred overnight, but divine love will not.

Let's look at Mark 11:23-25 in relation to faith working by the God-kind of love.

> **MARK 11:23,24**
> 23 For verily I say unto you, That whosoever shall say unto this mountain, Be thou removed, and be thou cast into the sea; and shall not doubt in his heart, but shall believe that those things which he saith shall come to pass; he shall have whatsoever he saith.
> 24 Therefore I say unto you, What things soever ye desire, when ye pray, believe that ye receive them, and ye shall have them.

Most Christians rejoice over Mark 11:23,24, and I personally thank God for these verses of scripture because they brought me off a deathbed almost sixty years ago. But let's read a little further in verse 25.

> **MARK 11:25**
> 25 And when ye stand praying, forgive, if ye have ought against any: that your Father also which is in heaven may forgive you your trespasses.

Verse 25 is as much a part of the Bible as Mark 11:23,24. Notice the conjunction "and" at the beginning of verse 25. The word "and" joins what Jesus said previously in verses 23 and 24 — that you can have what you say if you believe it in your heart — to what He said in verse 25: "*And when ye stand praying, FOR-GIVE. . . .*" Faith works by love, and divine love *forgives.*

Some folks say, "I just can't forgive So-and-so." But the God-kind of love *can* forgive. Really, if a believer says, "I just can't forgive," he is letting his head or flesh dominate him because the love of God has been shed abroad in his heart by the Holy Ghost (Rom. 5:5), and love forgives. Actually, the Bible says we as Christians can forgive just as God forgave us: *"And be ye kind one to another, tenderhearted, FORGIVING one another, EVEN AS God for Christ's sake hath forgiven you"* (Eph. 4:32).

I remember a woman in one of the churches I pastored who was an example of someone letting the flesh dominate instead of walking in love. My wife and I had just accepted the pastorate of this church. As we were moving into the parsonage, this woman came over and began talking to us.

The woman said, "Now, Brother Hagin, I know you are going to hear about this, so I want to tell you firsthand myself." (You'd better watch those folks who always want to give you *firsthand* information; that "firsthand information" is usually slanted in their favor.)

She continued, "I just wanted to tell you how old Sister So-and-so treated me." I listened to the woman for a while, but finally I stopped her and said, "Just wait a minute, Sister. When did this happen?" "Eight years ago next Tuesday," she said.

I was appalled, and I suppose she could tell I was because my mouth fell open, and my eyes bugged out. "Now don't misunderstand me. I've forgiven her," she said, "but I'll never forget how that old devil [speaking of this other woman] treated me."

Without thinking, I pointed my finger in her face

and said, "Sister, you're a bald-faced liar." She was
stunned. I said, "You haven't forgiven her because if you
had forgiven her, you wouldn't still be talking about it."
You see, love not only forgives, but it also *forgets*.

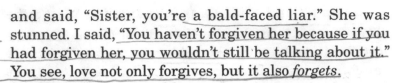

God didn't say, "I have forgiven you of your sins, but
every time I get a chance, I'm going to remind you of
them." If God did that, we'd all be in a mess. No, God
cancelled our sins because of Christ's substitutionary
work on the cross. God said in Isaiah 43:25: "*I, even I,
am he that blotteth out thy transgressions for mine own
sake, and WILL NOT REMEMBER thy sins.*"

We know that God is love. And love says, ". . . *their
sins and their iniquities will I remember no more*" (Heb.
8:12). What happens many times is that people let their
heads dominate them instead of their hearts. But the
Bible says the love of God is shed abroad in our *hearts*
(Rom. 5:5), not in our heads.

My wife and I were holding a meeting once in the
western part of the United States. After the meeting, a
young couple who were in the ministry invited us out to
eat. As we were seated in the restaurant, the woman
said to me, "Brother Hagin, you've gotten me confused."
She was referring to something I had said in the meeting.

This woman said, "In your message tonight, you
mentioned First John 3:14,15. When you got to the part
where it says, '*Whosoever hateth his brother is a murderer: and ye know that no murderer hath eternal life
abiding in him,*' you said, 'and that also means whosoever hateth his *mother-in-law* too!'"

I said, "Yes, I said that. I plead guilty. What's the problem? Why are you confused?"

"Well," she said, "I hate my mother-in-law."

I answered her, "If you do, you don't have eternal life abiding in you."

She argued, "But I got saved and was baptized in the Holy Ghost when I was just a little girl."

"I don't care how long you've been saved and filled with the Holy Ghost," I responded, "if you hate your mother-in-law, you don't have eternal life abiding in you. That's what the Bible says."

Now I knew she didn't really hate her mother-in-law. And I knew she was saved and Spirit-filled and that she loved God. I knew what had happened, but I just wanted her to see it. She had let her head dominate her in this area. She had let her head get between her and God, so to speak, and she had let the flesh take over. No, it wasn't a devil or a demon that had gotten ahold of her. It was just the flesh.

I said to this woman, "Look me right in the eye and say, 'I hate my mother-in-law,' and at the same time, check up in your spirit." She looked me in the eye and said, "I hate my mother-in-law."

I asked her, "What happened on the inside of you?" She said, "There's something down there scratching me."

"Yes," I said, "and that 'something' is trying to get your attention. The love of God has been shed abroad in your heart — in your spirit. The love of God is trying to get your attention."

She asked, "What am I going to do?"

I said, "Act like you would if you did love her, because you do. You've got to let the love of God that's been shed abroad in your heart express itself. And you do that by actions and by words."

It's the same way with faith. Faith is of the heart. You could have a heart full of faith and still die of sickness or disease. Or you could have a heart full of faith and never get an answer to prayer. You've got to *release* your faith or *express* your faith. You've got to get that faith out of your heart and into expression. You've got to get your faith working and active. How do you do that? Through actions and words.

The mother of a fifteen-year-old boy stopped me after a meeting once and said to me, "Brother Hagin, I want you to promise me something." "What is it?" I asked. She proceeded to explain that she was a widow who had only been saved a few years and now her son, who wasn't raised in church, was having some problems.

This mother said, "I can't do a thing with him. He stays out late at night, sometimes as late as four o'clock in the morning. I just lie awake at night and wait for the phone to ring and someone to tell me he's been arrested. I want you to promise me that you'll pray for him every day until he gets saved."

I answered this woman, "I'm not going to do it. I'm not going to make such a promise because I'm not going to pray for him every day."

"Well, then just pray for him when you think about it," she said.

I told her, "I'm not even going to pray for him at all."

That shocked her, but I said it to get her attention. "You're not?" she asked. "No," I said. "In fact, I'm not going to pray one single prayer for him." I added, "It wouldn't do any good even if I did pray."

"What do you mean?" she asked, bewildered.

I said, "It wouldn't do any good to pray as long as you keep condemning him. I dare say that you probably hassle him at every meal and constantly try to poke religion down him and push Jesus off on him."

This mother was stunned. "How did you know I did that?" she asked.

"Because of the way he turned out," I answered. "You've turned him off to the things of God by nagging at him. Now you promise me something."

"What is it?" she asked.

"Promise me that from this day forward you won't say one more word to him about Jesus," I answered. "Don't nag at him and don't invite him to go to church. Just act in love toward him. And when he's out at night, instead of lying awake and worrying, just say, 'Lord, I surround him with faith and love. No, I don't believe he's going to end up in reform school or in the penitentiary. I believe he's going to serve God.'"

"I'll try it," this mother agreed. "Trying it won't work," I said. "Just *do* it." She said, "All right, but you're still going to pray, aren't you?"

I said, "No, I'm not going to pray at all. You're going to do it. It's not up to me; it's up to you."

I went back to the same city for a meeting fifteen months later and this same woman came up to me after the meeting and shook hands with me. "Do you remember me?" she asked. "About fifteen months ago, I asked you to pray every day for my son." I hadn't recognized this woman at first because she looked so different — she looked younger. She said, "I did what you told me to do about my son. It was hard, but I did it."

The woman went on to relate: "About six months ago, my son came home at four o'clock one morning. It was Saturday night. On Sunday morning, I got up to make breakfast before going to Sunday school and church. My son got up and ate breakfast and said, 'Mom, I believe I'll go with you to Sunday school and church this morning.'

"I acted as though I didn't care if he went to church or not. In fact, I said, 'Are you sure you want to go this morning? You didn't get in until late this morning and you've got school tomorrow. You need your rest.' My son said, 'No, I want to go to church with you.'

"The next Saturday night he did the same thing. He went to church that Sunday morning and again Sunday night. And Sunday night when the altar call was given, he was born again and filled with the Holy Ghost."

The mother continued, "My son was living one hundred percent for the devil, but now he's living one hundred and twenty percent for God! I believe he's going to be a preacher. I'm so glad I did what you told me to do.

Not only do I have a brand-new boy, but my son has a brand-new momma!

"I don't ever worry about anything anymore because I learned how to pray in faith and to walk in love. Sometimes I have to pinch myself and say, *Is that really you?* because I think so differently now."

It makes a lot of difference, friends, when you walk in love. When you walk in love, your faith will work. If my faith wasn't working, that's the first thing I would check up on — to see if I was walking in love.

We know that faith works by love; in fact, faith won't work any other way. In other words, you could have faith to move mountains, but if you're not walking in love, your faith will be ineffective. You've got to release the love of God from your heart in the same way you release your faith — through actions and words — because faith and love are of the heart. *And faith works by love!*

Chapter 12
Six Hindrances to Faith

Fight the good fight of faith, lay hold on eternal life, whereunto thou art also called, and hast professed a good profession before many witnesses.

— 1 Timothy 6:12

I want you to notice particularly the first clause of this verse, *"Fight the good fight of faith. . . ."* The only fight believers fight is the good fight of faith. The Bible calls it a *good* fight of faith because Jesus whipped the devil at the Cross and rose a victor over him.

Sometimes I hear Christians say they are going to fight the devil. I don't know why they would want to do that because Jesus already defeated him for them. They wouldn't be a match for him anyway.

I also hear folks say, "I'm going to fight sin." Well, I'm not. I'm going to preach the *cure* for sin. There's no use fighting sin. There is a cure for sin. *Jesus* is the cure. No, the only fight the believer is called upon to fight is the good fight of faith.

The Bible says each believer has been given a measure of faith (Rom. 12:3). When you talk to some believers, they're always confessing their lack of faith. The truth is, they do have faith, but they may not have *developed* it, or they have failed to *release* it. In that

126

case, lack of faith is not the real problem.

If a believer doesn't develop his measure of faith, his faith will be weak. Weak faith is also caused by a lack of knowledge of God's Word, for ". . . *faith cometh by hearing, and hearing by the word of God"* (Rom. 10:17). You can't increase your faith any other way except through the Word.

Someone said, "I'm *praying* God will give me faith." Well, you are wasting your time. You might as well twiddle your thumbs and say, "Twinkle, twinkle, little star," because that's how much good it would do to pray for faith.

But if you'll take time to feed on the Word of God for yourself and listen to the many ministry gifts God has put in His Church, then faith will come into your spirit as you receive knowledge of the Word. A lack of knowledge of God's Word will hinder you and hold you in bondage. You cannot act upon God's Word beyond the knowledge you have of it.

Faith will grow with an understanding of the Word. If your faith is not growing, your understanding of the Word is not growing. A lack of knowledge of what God's Word says about your redemptive rights in Christ can keep you in a state of unbelief.

It's vitally important to feed upon the Word and allow your faith to grow so you can fight the good fight of faith. And notice it's a *fight* of faith. That means there must be *enemies* or *hindrances* to faith. If there weren't any enemies or hindrances to faith, there wouldn't be any fight to it. Let me give you six big hindrances to faith.

The first hindrance to faith is *a lack of understanding of what it means to be a new creation in Christ.* In Second Corinthians 5:17 it says, *"Therefore if any man be in Christ, he is a new creature: old things are passed away; behold, all things are become new."* A failure to understand what it means to be a new creature in Christ hinders our faith life.

Many people do not know they are new creatures. They think God just forgave them of their sins. But it wouldn't do any good for God just to forgive the sinner of his sins. It wouldn't help a sinner a bit in the world if forgiveness was all he received in the new birth. He would still go to hell, for unless his nature is changed, he would still be a child of the devil. A person has to be born again and receive a new *nature* in Christ. He has to become a new creature.

No, we are not just forgiven sinners. We are not just poor, staggering, sinning church members either. We are not living down at the end of the block on Barely-Get-Along Street next to Grumble Alley. That's not for us! We are new creatures, created by God in Christ Jesus, with the very life and nature of God in our spirits. We are children of God and joint heirs with Jesus Christ.

Many believers do not know they have eternal life. They think of themselves as being saved from sin, of course. But the Bible says, *"These things have I written unto you that believe on the name of the Son of God; that ye may know that YE HAVE ETERNAL LIFE . . ."*

(1 John 5:13). When you know what you possess because of your inheritance in Christ, and who you are in Christ, it makes all the difference in the world to your faith life.

The second hindrance to faith is *a lack of understanding of our place in Christ.* I suggest to Christians that they go through the New Testament, particularly the epistles, and write down all the scriptures which say, "In Christ," "In Whom," and "In Him."

You'll find these expressions occur 133 or 134 times in the New Testament. I include in that list verses that don't say these exact words but infer it.

For instance, I use First John 4:4, which says, *". . . greater is he that is in you, than he that is in the world."* I also use Colossians 1:13: *"Who* [God, the Father] *hath delivered us from the power of darkness, and hath translated us into the kingdom of his dear Son."*

As you go through the New Testament and find these "In Him" scriptures, you need to confess, "This is who I am in Christ," and "This is what I have in Christ." If you'll do that, you'll find life will be different for you.

The third hindrance to faith is *a lack of understanding of righteousness.* Failure to understand righteousness holds more people in bondage than anything else.

I will never forget when I first began to understand the scriptures on faith and healing years ago as I lay on the bed of sickness. I found James 5:16, which says, *". . . The effectual fervent prayer of a righteous man availeth much."* I looked at that verse and thought, *Oh my! If I were only righteous! If I could ever get to be righteous, God would hear my prayers.*

One day I happened to be reading that passage of Scripture a little more closely and noticed the Bible said Elijah was subject to like passions as we are (James 5:17). Yet it gave him as an example of a righteous man.

Something about that registered in me. I realized if Elijah could be called a righteous man, then I could, too, because I was a human being just as he was. Elijah had his high moments and his low moments. But I thought to myself, *How could God call a person like that righteous when he was so inconsistent?*

Then I read Psalm 32:2: *"Blessed is the man unto whom the Lord imputeth not iniquity. . . ."* Even under the Old Covenant, God imputed righteousness to those whose sins had been covered by the blood of sacrificial animals. And I read Second Corinthians 5:21: *"For he hath made him to be sin for us, who knew no sin; that we might be made the righteousness of God in him."*

The blood of Jesus doesn't just *cover* our sin. It cleanses us from all sin and in the new birth we become righteous new creatures in Christ. God doesn't make *un*righteous new creatures.

We are created by God in Christ Jesus. We are sons and daughters of God. We can stand in God's Presence as though we never sinned, without any kind of feeling of inferiority, sin-consciousness, or without any kind of embarrassment. We don't have to be tongue-tied because of fear. We can come into God's Presence because we belong there — He is our Heavenly Father.

When we were born again, our sins were remitted. The sins of our past life were blotted out by the blood of Jesus. God said He would not remember our transgressions anymore (Ps. 103:12; Isa. 43:25). If He doesn't remember them, why should we?

Some people say they have sinned a lot since they were saved, and that they are spiritually weak. But I have news for them. In First John 1:9 it says, *"If we confess our sins, he is faithful and just to forgive us our sins, and to CLEANSE US from all unrighteousness."*

God does two things for the believer when he asks forgiveness for missing it. First, when the believer confesses his sin, the Lord *forgives* him. Second, the Lord *cleanses* him from all unrighteousness.

When we sin, we feel guilty and have a sense of unrighteousness. We feel embarrassed and spiritually inferior to come into God's Presence. But God says when we confess our sins, He cleanses us from *all* unrighteousness. "Unrighteousness" is just the word "righteousness" with the prefix "un-" in front of it, meaning *not* or *non-righteous*. If we are cleansed from non-righteousness, then we are righteous again.

I find many times that when I get folks to see that they are righteous in Christ, they automatically get healed. Many times folks are under condemnation and think God is mad at them. They fail to understand they are the righteousness of God in Christ.

The fourth hindrance to faith is *a lack of under-*

standing of our right and privilege to use the Name of Jesus. Failure to use that Name holds us in bondage and gives us a sense of spiritual weakness. When we know what that Name will do for us, we can overcome Satan in every circumstance and enjoy the victory Jesus already provided for us.

Most Christians understand that the Name of Jesus can be used in prayer because Jesus said, "... *Whatsoever ye shall ask the Father IN MY NAME, he will give it you. Hitherto have ye asked nothing in my name: ask . . . that your joy may be full"* (John 16:23,24). But the Name of Jesus can also be used everywhere the Word indicates it can.

For instance, in Mark 16, Jesus said, *"And these signs shall follow them that believe; IN MY NAME shall they cast out devils; they shall speak with new tongues; . . . they shall lay hands on the sick, and they shall recover"* (vv. 17,18). These signs shall follow those that *believe* in the Lord Jesus Christ and *act* on their authority in Jesus' Name.

These signs are not just for the Early Church or the apostles or preachers. *Every* believer has authority over devils in the Name of Jesus. And in that mighty Name, every believer can lay hands on the sick, and the sick shall recover.

The fifth hindrance to faith is *a lack of understanding about acting on the Word.* We should stop *trying* to obey the Word and start *acting* on the Word! The Bible says, *"Trust in the Lord . . . and lean not unto thine own understanding"* (Prov. 3:5). Just ask, "What does God's

Word say?" If we know the Word is true and we act as though it is true, it becomes a reality in our lives.

6 The sixth hindrance to faith is *a lack of understanding that we are to hold fast to our confession of faith.* The truth is, our faith keeps pace with our confession.

HEBREWS 4:14
14 Seeing then that we have a great high priest, that is passed into the heavens, Jesus the Son of God, let us HOLD FAST OUR PROFESSION.

ROMANS 10:10
10 For with the heart man BELIEVETH unto righteousness; and with the mouth CONFESSION is made unto salvation.

MARK 11:23
23 ... whosoever shall SAY unto this mountain, Be thou removed, and be thou cast into the sea; and shall not doubt in his heart, but shall BELIEVE that those things which he SAITH shall come to pass; he shall have whatsoever he SAITH.

I was preaching in St. Louis once and the youth director of the church said to me, "Brother Hagin, I'm thirty-two years old and the doctors have said it is impossible for me and my wife to have any children. Will you pray with us?" I told him I would.

So I talked with him and his wife. The youth minister and his wife told me that from then on they would confess the Word of God over their situation. Then we agreed together in prayer. After twelve months I received a letter from this couple. They wrote me that they had a beautiful baby girl. All they had needed to do was to act on the Word.

Faith is measured by our confession. Our usefulness in the Lord is measured by our confession.

So study the Word for yourself and find out who you are in Christ and what you have in Christ. Hold fast to your confession of faith. Don't let anything hinder you from overcoming in your good fight of faith!

Chapter 13
The Mercies of God

The Lord is gracious, and full of compassion;
slow to anger, and of great mercy.
The Lord is good to all: and his tender mer-
cies are over all his works.

— Psalm 145:8,9

A wealth of information about the nature and character of God is revealed in these two verses of Scripture. The Lord is gracious, full of compassion, slow to
anger, *and* of great mercy. Verse 9 says the Lord is good
to all — not just to a few, but to *all* — and his mercies
are over all his works.

Our text says, *"The Lord is gracious, and full of*
compassion. . . ." The phrase, "full of compassion"
could also be translated *merciful*. In other words, many
times "mercy" and "compassion" are interchangeable
words in the Scriptures. To be merciful means to be full
of compassion. God is full of compassion, and the Bible
says He is of *great* mercy (Ps. 145:8).

PSALM 106:7
7 Our fathers understood not thy wonders in
Egypt; they remembered not THE MULTITUDE
OF THY MERCIES; but provoked him at the sea,
even at the Red sea.

God performed many signs and wonders when He

delivered the children of Israel out of Egypt. But this verse says the Israelites didn't understand God's miraculous works, nor did they remember the multitude of His mercies. You see, many people think of God's mercy only in relation to salvation for sinners. Thank God, His mercy *is* extended to sinners, and sinners *can* be saved if they will believe on and call on the Name of the Lord Jesus Christ.

However, there's more to God's mercy than just the provision of salvation for sinners. The psalmist said, *". . . they remembered not the MULTITUDE of thy mercies . . ."* (Ps. 106:7). What were the multitude of mercies God showed to the children of Israel? For one thing, God's mercies were shown in the wonders and miracles He performed in delivering the Israelites out of Egypt where they had been held captive. The psalmist called those wonders God's *mercies*.

PSALM 119:41
41 Let thy MERCIES come also unto me, O Lord, even thy salvation, according to thy word.

Notice again the word, "mercies," instead of "mercy." The writer is talking about mercies — *plural*. In other words, the psalmist wasn't just talking about the forgiveness of sins. He was talking about *all* of God's mercies, which also include all of God's provisions.

The Bible says the Lord never changes (Mal. 3:6; Heb. 13:8). He's the same now as He was in the Old Testament. And if God was gracious and merciful to the children of Israel, He will be gracious and merciful to

His born-again children today. To be merciful is the same as being full of compassion. And since God was full of compassion then, He will be full of compassion now, because God never changes.

PSALM 59:16
16 But I will sing of thy power; yea, I will sing aloud of THY MERCY in the morning: for thou hast been my defence and refuge in the day of my trouble.

We also know God's mercy encompasses more than just the forgiveness of sins because in Psalm 59:16, David called deliverance from his enemy, Saul, God's *mercy.* So we know God's deliverance is also a manifestation of His mercy. In this psalm, David was talking about deliverance from Saul, but I don't know of a more cruel enemy to mankind than Satan, sin, sickness, and disease.

HEBREWS 4:16
16 Let us therefore come boldly unto the throne of grace, THAT WE MAY OBTAIN MERCY, and find grace to help in time of need.

If we're not careful, we will interpret this verse only in light of the forgiveness of sins. Certainly, if we sin or fail, God's mercy is available to restore us. God will have mercy on us and forgive us if we repent for our sins and ask for His forgiveness.

But we can see from the other scriptures we read that God's mercy encompasses more than just the forgiveness of sins. God's mercy encompasses material and physical provisions as well as spiritual blessings. When the scripture said, *"Let us therefore come boldly unto the throne of grace, that we may obtain mercy . . ."* (Heb. 4:16), it wasn't just talking about receiving forgiveness. It was also talking about obtaining healing, strength, help, deliverance in time of trouble, or *whatever* it is we need from God.

> **2 CORINTHIANS 1:3**
> **3　Blessed be God, even the Father of our Lord Jesus Christ, THE FATHER OF MERCIES, and the God of all comfort.**

In the New Testament we see again that God is the Father of *mercies,* not just the Father of *mercy.* If God's mercy only included the forgiveness of sins, then God would be the God of mercy. But, thank God, He is the God of *mercies*, and *all* of His mercies are available to us today!

> **2 CHRONICLES 16:9**
> **9　For the eyes of the Lord run to and fro throughout the whole earth, to shew himself strong in the behalf of them whose heart is perfect toward him. . . .**

God's eyes can see throughout the whole earth! And the Bible says the eyes of the Lord run to and fro throughout the whole earth so He can show Himself strong in behalf of those whose hearts are perfect toward Him. Many people have the wrong impression about the nature and character of God because of the lack of correct teaching.

In other words, many people imagine God as some mean fellow sitting up in Heaven with a big flyswatter, so to speak. They think the minute they make a mistake or a wrong move, God is going to swat them!

But the Bible says the eyes of the Lord run to and fro throughout the whole earth *". . . TO SHEW HIMSELF STRONG in the behalf of them whose heart is perfect toward him . . ."* (2 Chron. 16:9).

The eyes of the Lord run to and fro throughout the earth so He can show himself strong on behalf of people, not swat them like flies every time they make a mistake! God is the God of *mercies.* Our text says, *"The Lord is gracious, and full of compassion; slow to anger, and of great mercy. The Lord is good to all: and his tender mercies are over all his works"* (Ps. 145:8,9)!

If you want to know the character of God, look at Jesus. Jesus said, *". . . he that hath seen me hath seen the Father . . ."* (John 14:9). Looking at the miracles of Jesus in the Gospels, we see over and over again how Jesus was moved with compassion toward suffering humanity. Healing, too, is a manifestation of God's mercy.

MARK 1:40,41
40 And there came a leper to him [Jesus], beseeching him, and kneeling down to him, and saying unto him, If thou wilt, thou canst make me clean.
41 And Jesus, MOVED WITH COMPASSION [or mercy], put forth his hand, and touched him, and saith unto him, I will; be thou clean.

In Mark 1:41 it says that Jesus was moved with

compassion and healed the leper. The word "compassion" could also mean *pity* or *tender mercy.* One dictionary definition of "mercy" is *a blessing that is an act of divine favor or compassion.* In other words, compassion or mercy was what motivated Jesus to heal that leper and make him clean again.

> MATTHEW 20:29-34
> 29 And as they departed from Jericho, a great multitude followed him.
> 30 And, behold, two blind men sitting by the way side, when they heard that Jesus passed by, cried out, saying, HAVE MERCY ON US, O Lord, thou son of David.
> 31 And the multitude rebuked them, because they should hold their peace: but they cried the more, saying, HAVE MERCY ON US, O Lord, thou son of David.
> 32 And Jesus stood still, and called them, and said, What will ye that I shall do unto you?
> 33 They say unto him, Lord, that our eyes may be opened.
> 34 So Jesus HAD COMPASSION ON THEM, and touched their eyes: and immediately their eyes received sight, and they followed him.

Notice these two blind men asked Jesus for mercy. Then Jesus asked them, "...*What will ye that I shall do unto you?*" (Matt. 20:32), and they replied, "... *Lord, that our eyes may be opened*" (v. 33). And Jesus responded by granting them the mercy of healing!

If you will begin to see healing as a mercy of God and not try to base obtaining healing on works or on anything else but your faith in God's *mercy,* you will make progress in your Christian walk with God.

Remember the Bible says, *"The Lord is good to all: and his tender mercies are over all his works"* (Ps. 145:9). Are you one of God's "works"? The Bible says you are if you are in Christ (Eph. 2:10). If you are God's workmanship — one of God's works — then the Bible says His mercy is over you.

PSALM 145:8
8   The Lord is GRACIOUS, and full of compassion; slow to anger, and of GREAT MERCY.

The word "gracious" in this verse comes from the Hebrew word meaning *to show favor.* In other words when it says, *"The Lord is gracious . . ."* (v. 8), it is also saying, "The Lord is disposed or inclined to show favor." To show favor is part of God's disposition or character. It is God's disposition to be gracious, to be full of compassion, to be slow to anger, and to be of *great* mercy.

We read examples of the manifestation of God's mercy in the New Testament in the healing of the leper and of the two blind men. Let's look at another manifestation of God's mercy in the Old Testament.

2 CHRONICLES 5:12-14
12 . . . the Levites which were the singers . . . arrayed in white linen, having cymbals and psalteries and harps, stood at the east end of the altar, and with them an hundred and twenty priests sounding with trumpets:
13 It came even to pass, as the trumpeters and singers were as one, to make one sound to be heard in praising and thanking the Lord; and

> **when they lifted up their voice with the trumpets
> and cymbals and instruments of musick, and
> praised the Lord, saying, FOR HE IS GOOD; FOR
> HIS MERCY ENDURETH FOR EVER: that then
> the house was filled with a cloud, even the house
> of the Lord;**
> **14 So that the priests could not stand to minister
> by reason of the cloud: for the glory of the Lord
> had filled the house of God.**

Notice the trumpeters and singers were as one praising and thanking the Lord. What did they say as they praised and thanked God? They lifted up their voices, saying, ". . . *For he is good; for HIS MERCY ENDURETH FOR EVER* . . ." (2 Cor. 5:13). In singing God's praises, they extolled God's goodness and His mercy. And since God never changes, He is still good and merciful today.

The Bible says about God, ". . . *with whom is no variableness, neither shadow of turning*" (James 1:17). That's why we can say His mercy endures *forever!* We should praise and thank God for His goodness and mercy just as the children of Israel did.

If you'll read through the Psalms, which was the Israelites' prayer and songbook, you'll see how the psalmists constantly wrote about God's goodness and mercy. They constantly magnified this aspect of God's nature and character. What happens when you magnify God's goodness and mercy?

We read in Second Chronicles 5:12-14 that when the Israelites began to praise and thank the Lord, their praises brought a manifestation of God's glory and

power. In verse 13, the Bible says the glory of the Lord
filled the temple like a cloud.

2 CHRONICLES 5:13,14
13 . . . then the house WAS FILLED WITH A
CLOUD, even the house of the Lord;
14 So that the priests could not stand to minister
by reason of the cloud: FOR THE GLORY OF THE
LORD HAD FILLED THE HOUSE OF GOD.

Many times in my own meetings I have found that
in magnifying God's mercy, especially His healing
mercy, I would see the glory of God just as the Israelites
did in these verses. I would see the glory cloud in the
back of the auditorium come rolling in like ocean
waves.

I particularly remember one meeting I held in Col-
orado when the glory cloud was evident. I was ministering to the sick by the laying on of hands when suddenly
I saw a cloud come rolling into the auditorium. I knew
from the Scriptures and from experience that it was the
glory of God. So I stopped ministering to the people and
stepped back onto the platform.

The people who were in the healing line had their
eyes closed so they didn't see the cloud. When that
cloud moved directly over them, I just waved my hand
to one side, and everyone in that line fell under the
power of God like dominoes going down in a row.

However, the Spirit of God didn't minister just to
those who were in the healing line. The glory of God
filled that entire auditorium. After I closed that meeting and came back to Tulsa, I received a letter from a

woman who had attended the meeting with her husband. She said her husband had had a severe heart condition, and that heart specialists had told them, medically speaking, he was beyond help. Doctors could do nothing more for this man, and they said he wouldn't live much longer because of the heart disease.

This woman went on to relate that her husband didn't want to attend the meeting, but she just kept after him until he finally agreed to attend. They arrived at the meeting late and sat in the balcony of the auditorium.

The woman wrote, "Almost the entire time you were preaching, my husband kept saying out loud, 'I don't believe a word of it! There's nothing to it.' People sitting around us kept telling him to be quiet, and I just bowed my head and prayed. Then, Brother Hagin, when you started praying for people, my husband kept saying, 'That's nothing but hypnotism! He's just hypnotizing those people.'"

The woman said she just continued to pray quietly for her husband. She wrote, "When you stepped back onto the platform and waved your hand and the people started falling under the power of God, my husband said, 'It's going all over me! It's going all over me!'" She asked him, "What's going all over you?" He answered, "That power he's talking about! That anointing! It's going all over me." Glory to God, that man was healed by God's healing mercy!

Someone asked, "Why did that sinner man who was griping and complaining get healed?" The answer is very simple: The Bible says Christ died for the ungodly (Rom. 5:6), and this man qualified! Praise God for God's mercy. God's mercy reached out to this man and got through to him.

This man went back to the heart specialist for an examination, and the heart specialist told him, "Somebody up there likes you because you've got a brand-new heart!"

The woman who wrote me the letter, said, "My husband is a brand-new man. He's not only new physically because God healed his heart, but he's also new spiritually! He's been born again!"

You see, you can't come in contact with the mercy of God without His mercy affecting your life. And, thank God, His mercy reaches every area of our lives. The Lord is good to all, and His mercies are over all His works!

The Bible says, ". . . *I am the Lord, I change not . . .*" (Mal. 3:6), and *"Jesus Christ the same yesterday, and to day, and for ever"* (Heb. 13:8). What God did for His people in the Old Testament, He will do for His people today. God's mercies are extended to us, but we make it possible for Him to bless us by coming to Him in faith (Heb. 11:6).

Through faith in God and in His holy written Word, you can receive the mercies of God which include forgiveness of sins, healing for your body, and deliverance from anything that would bind or oppress you.

When you come in contact with God, you come in contact with His mercies. And you can receive whatever it is you need from your Heavenly Father because God is the Father of *mercies!*

Chapter 14
The Anointing Breaks the Yoke

... and THE YOKE SHALL BE DESTROYED
because of the ANOINTING.
— Isaiah 10:27

The anointing the Bible is talking about here is the manifest power of the Holy Spirit. We can learn an important principle regarding how the anointing works by following the ministry of Jesus. For instance, in Mark chapter 5 we see an illustration of the healing anointing in demonstration in the case of the woman with the issue of blood.

> **MARK 5:25-34**
> **25** And a certain woman, which had an issue of blood twelve years,
> **26** And had suffered many things of many physicians, and had spent all that she had, and was nothing bettered, but rather grew worse,
> **27** When she had heard of Jesus, came in the press behind, and touched his garment.
> **28** For she said, If I may touch but his clothes, I shall be whole.
> **29** And straightway the fountain of her blood was dried up; and she felt in her body that she was healed of that plague.
> **30** And Jesus, immediately knowing in himself that VIRTUE had gone out of him, turned him about in the press, and said, Who touched my clothes?

31 And his disciples said unto him, Thou seest the multitude thronging thee, and sayest thou, Who touched me?
32 And he looked round about to see her that had done this thing.
33 But the woman fearing and trembling, knowing what was done in her, came and fell down before him, and told him all the truth.
34 And he said unto her, Daughter, thy FAITH hath made thee whole; go in peace, and be whole of thy plague.

There are two pivotal words in this account of the healing of the woman with the issue of blood. Those words are "virtue" and "faith." The Greek word "virtue" is translated *dunamis* or *miraculous power*.

Jesus, knowing immediately that virtue or power had gone out of Him, looked around and asked, "Who touched My clothes?" Then Jesus turned around and saw who had touched Him, and said to the woman, *". . . Daughter, THY FAITH hath made thee whole . . ."* (Mark 5:34).

Some people say, "I thought the power that flowed out of Jesus — the healing anointing — made that woman whole!" But Jesus said, "Daughter, *your faith has made you whole.*" Why did Jesus say that?

Years ago I heard a professor at a well-known university say, "In discussing Bible truths, very often it is like climbing a mountain. You climb up one side of the mountain and you see one view. You climb up the other side of the mountain and you see another view, but it is the same mountain. Which view is right? It depends upon which side of the mountain you're looking at."

Bible truth is that way too. From one viewpoint, it *was* the healing virtue coming forth from Jesus that effected the healing in this woman's body. However, on the other hand, it was her *faith* that received her healing because it was only when her faith *activated* the healing anointing that it broke the yoke of bondage — the sickness in her body.

When Jesus asked, "Who touched My clothes?" the disciples said to Jesus, ". . . *Thou seest the multitude thronging thee, and sayest thou, Who touched me?*" (Mark 5:31). In other words, they were saying, "How can You ask who touched You when so many people touched You?"

You know yourself if you were in a crowd of people where everyone was pressing in upon you, you'd get touched on every side. But the power of God isn't activated by just the *incidental* touch.

Then, too, I'm sure some people reached through the throng and touched Jesus out of curiosity to see if anything would happen, and nothing did. The power of God also isn't activated by the *curious* touch. No, Jesus said, ". . . *Daughter, THY FAITH hath made thee whole . . .*" (Mark 5:34). It's the touch of *faith* that releases the power of God to flow!

We know Jesus was anointed with power, because Acts 10:38 says, "*How God ANOINTED Jesus of Nazareth with the Holy Ghost and with POWER. . . .*" Then we also read where Jesus said, "*The Spirit of the Lord is upon me, because he hath ANOINTED me . . .*"

(Luke 4:18). In that same passage, Jesus said, ". . . *This day is this scripture fulfilled in your ears"* (Luke 4:21). In other words, Jesus was saying, "I am anointed."

So we know Jesus was anointed or *empowered* by the Holy Spirit, yet most of the time He didn't heal people by the anointing alone. For the most part, the other person's faith was also involved.

As you read the four Gospels carefully, not one time will you find where Jesus ever said to anyone, "According to *My* faith be it done unto you." Not one single time did Jesus say to anyone, "According to the *apostles'* faith be it done unto you." But as we saw in this account of the woman with the issue of blood, again and again Jesus said, "According to *your* faith be it done unto you" (Matt. 8:13; 9:29; 15:28; Mark 10:52).

We need to realize that God is present everywhere. Because He is present everywhere, so is His power. His power may not be in manifestation, but it is there.

Why doesn't God's power come into manifestation in every circumstance to heal every sick person? It doesn't for the simple reason that it takes someone exercising *faith* to release or activate the power or anointing. You see, the power of God is inactive, passive, or inert *until faith is exercised.* But once God's power is activated, it will break every yoke.

This same principle of activating a power source applies in the natural realm. For instance, plugging a fan into an electrical outlet on a hot summer day activates the power of electricity and causes the fan to cool the air.

However, if no one plugs in the fan, the fan won't work and the room stays hot. In that case, the power of electricity is *present* and *available* to cool the room, but it isn't being *utilized* or *activated*. In order to tap into the power and cool the room, someone has to plug in the fan!

I learned this principle of releasing God's power through faith the hard way as a young boy on the bed of sickness. I was bedfast for sixteen long months. During those months, the healing power of God was present to heal me. But I wasn't healed because I didn't know how to exercise my faith and activate the power. However, I finally began to understand what Mark 11:24 was saying: ". . . *What things soever ye desire, when ye pray, believe that ye receive them, and ye shall have them.*"

I had been praying the entire sixteen months that I would be healed. A person can do a lot of praying when he's flat on his back for sixteen months! I prayed and cried and cried and prayed over and over again, waiting for God to heal me. I thought once I was entirely healed — once my heart was beating right, my paralysis was gone, and my blood disease was healed — *then* I'd believe I was healed.

But one day as I read Mark 11:24, I realized that my thinking was not in line with what the Bible teaches. I saw that Mark 11:24 was saying, "When ye pray, *believe you receive* (whatever it is you need from God) and *then* you will have it."

I desired to have a healed body. So when I saw what Mark 11:24 was really saying, I said out loud, "I see it! While I am still lying here flat on my back with my heart not beating right, my body still paralyzed, and with this incurable blood disease, I must begin to believe I receive healing!" (한글로 처방에도를 기쁘니!)

When I saw this in the Scriptures, I began to say out loud: "I believe I receive healing for the deformed heart. I believe I receive healing for the paralysis. I believe I receive healing for the incurable blood disease. I believe I receive healing from the top of my head to the soles of my feet."

I had never heard of anyone doing that. I was just following the Holy Spirit's leading and the Word of God. I had never heard anyone in my life say, "Praise the Lord" or "Glory to God," but from the inside of me I had an urge to praise and magnify God. I began to say, "Thank You, Lord, for my healing. Thank You, God, my heart is well. Thank You, God, my paralysis is healed. Thank You, God, the blood disease is healed."

As I did that, from the inside of me (because if you're born again, God is living in you) I heard, "Now you believe you're healed." I said, "I sure do!" Then that inward voice, which we sometimes call the still small voice, said, "Then get up. Healed people ought to be up at 10:30 in the morning."

When I heard the Holy Spirit say that, my head wanted to take over. My mental reasoning wanted to demand, "How is a paralyzed person going to get up?" But instead I made an effort. I managed to push myself to a seated position. I managed to push my feet off the bed and drape myself around the bedpost, wrapping my arms around it. I didn't have complete use of my arms, so there I was — no visible change — just draped around that bedpost.

Then I said out loud, "I want to announce in the presence of Almighty God, the Lord Jesus Christ, the Holy Spirit, all the holy angels who may be present in this room, and the devil and any evil spirits present in this room that according to Mark 11:24, I believe I receive healing for my body!"

When I said that, I felt something strike the top of my head. It was the power of the Holy Spirit. It felt like someone was standing above me pouring a pitcher of warm honey over my head. That warm glow oozed down over my head, down my body and arms, and out the end of my toes and fingertips.

Until then I'd had some use of the upper part of my body, but from the waist down I'd had no feeling whatsoever. I didn't know my feet were down there unless I looked down and saw them. But when that warm glow slowly flowed throughout my body, all feeling returned.

As the power of God went out the ends of my toes, it felt to me like there were ten million pins pricking my legs. You can imagine how your legs would feel if you had been bedfast sixteen months, and all of a sudden you stood up and all the feeling in your legs returned.

So there I was, standing up straight beside my bed, with every symptom of sickness gone! The power of God had been in that room the entire sixteen months I was bedfast. I just hadn't known how to plug into it by faith!

Let's go back to the example of the fan. You can imagine how strange it would be for someone to say, "I have a fan to cool this room. It's not plugged in, but I'm just waiting for the electricity to make this fan work!"

That fan is not going to work until someone plugs it in! The electricity is already there; someone just needs to tap into it to activate it. It was the same way with my healing. I just needed to tap into the power of God that was already available and activate it by faith in His Word! When faith is mixed with the power of God, the anointing breaks every yoke!

If people only realized it, there is enough power — more than enough power — in every sick room to heal anyone who needs healing. We can see an example of this in Jesus' ministry in Luke chapter 5.

LUKE 5:17
17 And it came to pass on a certain day, as he was teaching, that there were Pharisees and doctors of the law sitting by, which were come out of every town of Galilee, and Judaea, and Jerusalem: and THE POWER OF THE LORD WAS PRESENT TO HEAL THEM.

Notice two things. First, the power of the Lord was present to heal people. Jesus was anointed with that power.

Second, notice that even though the power of the Lord was present to heal people, it doesn't mention one single person getting healed. The only person the Bible records being healed in this account was the paralyzed man who was lowered through the roof of the house by his four friends (Luke 5:18,19). And the Bible says Jesus healed that paralyzed man because He saw *their faith* (Luke 5:20-25).

The faith of the four men, plus the faith of the paralyzed man, activated the power of God to effect a healing and a cure in the man's body and the paralyzed man immediately rose up healed!

That's where some Christians have missed it. They've thought, *We don't have the anointing. That's the reason we're not receiving from God.* No, they had the power of God all the time; they just didn't mix any faith with it. They just didn't know how to tap into the power that was already available to them.

The power of God won't do a thing in the world by itself. It's inactive, inert, and passive until faith is mixed with it — until someone taps into it by believing and acting upon God's Word! You see, faith gives action to the anointing or the power of God. If there is no faith to give action to the anointing, nothing will happen!

Whatever you are believing God for, mix faith with it! Exercise your faith and watch God work on your behalf as His anointing breaks every yoke of bondage!

Chapter 15
The Name of Jesus and You

Verily, verily, I say unto you, He that believeth on me, the works that I do shall he do also; and greater works than these shall he do; because I go unto my Father.

And whatsoever ye shall ASK in my name, that will I do, that the Father may be glorified in the Son.

If ye shall ASK any thing in my name, I will do it.

— John 14:12-14

Jesus told the disciples, *"If ye shall ASK any thing in my name, I WILL DO IT"* (John 14:14). *Strong's Exhaustive Concordance* brings out one meaning of the word "ask" here. This Greek word for "ask" implies *a demand of something due.*[1] Jesus was talking about *using His Name as a basis for authority* to demand our rightful inheritance in Christ.

Jesus wasn't saying you are to demand of *God*. God doesn't withold any good thing from His children. He was saying you are to demand that *Satan* cease and desist in his operations against you in the Name of Jesus. You are to exercise your authority over Satan and circumstances that are contrary to God's Word. And you are to speak forth the command of faith in Jesus' mighty Name.

155

Acts 3 records an account of Peter and John asking or demanding in Jesus' Name according to John 14:13,14. Notice in this passage that the disciples didn't pray. They exercised their rightful authority in Jesus' Name.

ACTS 3:2-8
2 And a certain man lame from his mother's womb was carried, whom they laid daily at the gate of the temple which is called Beautiful, to ask alms of them that entered into the temple;
3 Who seeing Peter and John about to go into the temple asked an alms.
4 And Peter, fastening his eyes upon him with John, said, Look on us.
5 And he game heed unto them, expecting to receive something of them.
6 Then Peter said, Silver and gold have I none; but such as I have give I thee: IN THE NAME OF JESUS CHRIST of Nazareth RISE UP AND WALK.
7 And he took him by the right hand, and lifted him up: and immediately his feet and ancle bones received strength.
8 And he leaping up stood, and walked, and entered with them into the temple, walking, and leaping, and praising God.

Peter didn't demand anything of *God* when he commanded, ". . . *In the name of Jesus Christ of Nazareth rise up and walk*" (v. 6). Why didn't he? Because God never made that man crippled to begin with — *Satan* did.

Peter demanded that the man arise and walk in Jesus' Name! He used the Name of Jesus to set the crippled man free from the bondage of Satan. Acts 3:16 says, "*And HIS NAME through faith in HIS NAME*

hath made this man strong, whom ye see and know: yea,
the faith which is by him hath given him this perfect
soundness. . . ." It is the Name of Jesus which gives the
believer the authority over the devil and guarantees the
answer to the command of faith!

Notice what Paul says in his letter to the Philippian
church about the Name of Jesus.

PHILIPPIANS 2:9-11
9 Wherefore God also hath highly exalted him,
and given him A NAME which is above every
name:
10 That at THE NAME OF JESUS every knee
should bow, of things in heaven, and things in
earth, and things under the earth;
11 And that every tongue should confess that
Jesus Christ is Lord, to the glory of God the
Father.

Verse 10 says ". . . *every knee should bow, of things*
in heaven, and things in earth, and things under the
earth." Other translations say "beings" instead of
"things." So we could read verse 10, ". . . every knee
should bow, of beings in Heaven, and beings in earth,
and beings under the earth."

Beings in Heaven, in the earth, and under the earth
include angels and demons. In other words, angels and
demons alike are subject to the Name of Jesus. They
must surrender to that Name because the Name of
Jesus is superior to every name that can be named in
three realms: Heaven, earth, and under the earth!

As Christians, the Name of Jesus belongs to us.

Many times, His Name doesn't mean as much to us as it should. Often our thinking is all wrong on this subject.

If your thinking is wrong, your believing will be wrong. And if your believing is wrong, then your speaking will be wrong too. It all goes back to your thinking. You've got to get your thinking straightened out before the Name of Jesus will mean what it *should* mean to you.

The Bible says, "*. . . faith cometh by hearing, and hearing by the word of God*" (Rom. 10:17). You've got to have *faith* in the Name of Jesus before that Name will produce results for you. When your faith in the Name of Jesus increases, results will also increase when you ask in His Name.

Many Christians think of the Name of Jesus in the same way they think of a good luck charm. They have about as much faith in the Name of Jesus as they have in a rabbit's foot!

These Christians say, "Maybe asking in Jesus' Name will work," or "I sure hope something good comes out of asking in that Name."

As long as you just *try* the Name of Jesus like it's some sort of a good luck charm, nothing will happen for you. The only way you will ever see any results is if God in His mercy intervenes on your behalf and does something for you in spite of yourself.

You need to get a revelation in your spirit that the Name of Jesus *belongs* to you as a Christian. You have a *right* to use that Name. When sickness or disease tries to attack you, you can demand, "In the Name of

Jesus Christ, leave my body!"

That's how I've been able to live for nearly sixty years without having a headache. I didn't say headache symptoms never tried to attack me. I said I haven't had a headache in nearly sixty years because when a symptom came, I demanded that it leave in Jesus' Name, and it left!

If symptoms of sickness or disease try to attack your body, don't just accept them and go around talking about your troubles with others. Instead say, "In the Name of Jesus Christ of Nazareth, sickness and disease, leave my body!" When you exercise your authority by faith in the Name of Jesus, sickness or disease must go!

"Well," you may say, "I tried that and it didn't work." Using the Name of Jesus doesn't work by *trying* it; it works by *doing* it. But you must have faith in that Name before it will work for you. And you must *exercise* your rightful authority in that Name before it will work for you.

Your spirit man — the real you on the inside — is the ruler of your body. In other words, *you* are the ruler or the caretaker of your own body. And *you* are the one who must exercise dominion over it in Jesus' Name — not someone else.

I once read about a man who was the caretaker of some landscaped government property in the state of Washington. After repeated efforts to stop people from walking on the grass, this caretaker posted a sign which read, "Gentlemen *will not*, and others *must not* trespass on this property."

When Satan tries to attack your body with sickness or disease, stop him in Jesus' Name. Tell him, "Satan, you *will not* trespass on my body with your symptoms of sickness or disease. In the Name of Jesus, you *must* go!"

You see, *you* — not someone else — are the caretaker of *your* body. You have a right to forbid Satan to trespass against your body with sickness or disease in the Name of Jesus!

When you take authority over sickness or disease in your body and command it to leave in Jesus' Name, you are demanding something due you — freedom from whatever symptoms have tried to attack your body. John 14:14 says, *"If ye shall ask* [or demand] *any thing in my name, I will do it."*

Remember, you're not demanding anything of God. You're demanding that demon forces stop in their operations against you, because sickness and disease come from the devil, not from God. You are exercising your scriptural authority over the devil in Jesus' Name.

Jesus told the disciples to pray that God's will would be done on earth as it is in Heaven (Matt. 6:10). There isn't any sickness in Heaven and God doesn't want you to be sick here on earth. When you take authority over sickness or disease in your body in the Name of Jesus, you're just taking your place as a child of God with certain rights and privileges in Christ. You're just exercising your rightful authority as Jesus told you to do in His Word!

We not only have to exercise authority over the

devil, we also have to exercise authority over our own
bodies. The Apostle Paul said, ". . . *I keep under my*
body, and BRING IT INTO SUBJECTION: lest that by
any means, when I have preached to others, I myself
should be a castaway" (1 Cor. 9:27).

To bring something into subjection is to take authority over it. Paul said he brought his body into subjection. In other words, he exercised authority over it to
make it line up with the Word of God.

Some Christians don't bring their bodies into subjection. They are *carnal* or *body-ruled*. Yet every Christian
has the ability to bring his or her body into subjection
as Paul did.

Just because Paul was an apostle, doesn't mean he
was any more saved than you are. He didn't have any
more authority over his body than you do over yours.
But he *exercised* his authority. *He* brought his body into
subjection.

ROMANS 12:1
1   I beseech you therefore, brethren, by the mer-
cies of God, that ye PRESENT YOUR BODIES A
LIVING SACRIFICE, holy, acceptable unto God,
which is your reasonable service.

One translation of this verse says, "which is your
spiritual service." Paul said presenting your body as a
living sacrifice is your spiritual service. That applies to
every believer.

You are the ruler of your own body. If you weren't
the ruler of your own body, you couldn't bring it into

subjection, and you couldn't present it to God as a living sacrifice. If you weren't the ruler of your body, you wouldn't be able to take authority over sickness or disease that might try to harm you.

But you *are* the ruler of your own body! And, thank God, you have the right to live free from the bondage of sin, pain, sickness, and disease in the Name of Jesus! However, you must *exercise* the authority which belongs to you *in that Name.*

Many times Christians don't understand the authority they have in the Name of Jesus. They have been religiously brainwashed instead of New Testament taught to think that they don't have a say-so about *anything* that happens to them. Rather than *dominating* their circumstances, some Christians *are being dominated* by their circumstances.

We don't know the authority God has given us as we should. Or if we do know it, we don't always exercise our authority as we should. We need to meditate upon the scriptures which tell us who we are in Christ and the authority God has given us in the Name of Jesus.

The Name of Jesus won't work for you just because you saw someone else use it. That Name won't work for you as it should until you apply yourself to study its meaning and its worth. You must be convinced of the Word of God for yourself and then act on the Word because *you* believe it's true. You need to *know* the authority God has given you in Jesus' Name, *believe* in that authority, and *exercise* it.

When you understand the authority you have in the

Name of Jesus, you can also use that Name to break the power of the devil over unsaved people, particularly your unsaved loved ones. I used the Name of Jesus for years, commanding sickness or pain or whatever tried to come against me to leave. As I used that Name, the symptoms left my body. But then I began to see that I could use Jesus' Name to break the power of the devil over my loved ones and claim their salvation.

One day the Holy Spirit said to me in my spirit, "No one in his right mind would drive his automobile one hundred miles per hour past flashing red lights and signs that read, 'Warning! Bridge Out!' without stopping his automobile in order to avoid destruction. But a person who *was not* in his right mind would!"

A drunk person, for example, is not in his right mind. A drunk person is not as alert as someone who is sober and, consequently, he might not heed the red flashing lights and warning signs. The Bible says, *". . . the god of this world hath BLINDED THE MINDS of them which BELIEVE NOT, lest the light of the glorious gospel of Christ, who is the image of God, should shine unto them"* (2 Cor. 4:4).

As the Holy Spirit spoke to me about this, I could see in the Spirit a multitude of people going down what appeared to be a highway. The multitude came to a place where the highway ended, and they plunged over what looked like the edge of a cliff and fell down into the pit of hell! The god of this world, Satan, had blinded their minds.

After this vision, I realized that sometimes you'll

have to break the power of the devil over a person's life because the person is being hindered from accepting Jesus.

The Word says, *"The entrance of thy words giveth light; it giveth understanding unto the simple"* (Ps. 119:130). When you expose a person to the Word, the Word gives him light spiritually so he can see the truth. But sometimes the power which is controlling an unsaved person needs to be broken or rendered ineffective before he can see the truth and act on it.

I saw that I could use the authority in the Name of Jesus break the power of the devil that was blinding my loved ones to the truth. So I immediately said, "I take the Name of Jesus and break the power of the devil over my brother, Dub, and I claim his deliverance and salvation."

My brother Dub was the "black sheep" of the family. When I took authority over the demons influencing his life and then claimed his salvation, that settled it for me. I didn't even think about it or pray about it anymore. I didn't even know where he was at the time I used the Name of Jesus on his behalf, but to me it was settled. And within three weeks, Dub was saved!

You must use the Name of Jesus in faith, otherwise you will be ineffective and you won't get results. Unbelief cries and begs and pleads, but faith *speaks* and then shouts the victory!

Jesus said, *"If ye shall ask* [demand] *any thing in*

my name, I will do it" (John 14:14). I didn't get the revelation of that scripture just by reading it once or twice; I didn't get it by hearing someone else's testimony of how it worked for him. I got the revelation of the power of the Name of Jesus by careful *study, meditation,* and *application* of the truth.

Someone might say, "Well, I don't know about that. I *tried* using the Name of Jesus once and it didn't work." Once the authority that's in the Name of Jesus has dawned on you and becomes a reality in your spirit, your days of *trying* will be over and your days of *doing* will begin! Then *no one* will be able to steal that revelation from you.

In order to live the abundant life God has provided for us, each of us needs to clearly understand the power and the authority that's in the Name of Jesus, as well as our right to use that Name.

So meditate upon the scriptures which tell you who you are in Christ and reveal the authority you have as a believer. As you do, those scriptures will become a reality to you, and you will begin to exercise your right to live in complete deliverance from the bondage of Satan in the Name of Jesus!

---

1 James Strong, *Strong's Exhaustive Concordance,* Greek Dictionary of the New Testament, p. 9 (154) and p. 63 (4441, compare reference to 154).

Chapter 16
Plead Your Case

I, even I, am he that blotteth out thy transgressions for mine own sake, and will not remember thy sins.

Put me in remembrance: let us plead together: declare thou [set forth thy cause], that thou mayest be justified.

— Isaiah 43:25,26

Someone once said, "It is more important that men learn to pray than it is for them to gain a college education." Notice, it's not that a college education is not important; but learning to pray is *more* important. People go to great effort and expense to gain a college education. It's not expensive to learn to pray, but it may require some effort!

I feel so sorry for folks who don't know how to plead their case with God in the crises of life or as needs arise. They may know how to say words. But there is a vast difference between just spouting words off into the air and effective prayer that obtains needed answers.

Prayer is joining forces with God the Father. It is fellowshipping with Him. It is carrying out His will upon the earth.

John Wesley, founder of the Methodist denomination, said, "It seems that God is limited by our prayer life. He can do nothing for humanity unless someone asks Him to do it."

You might ask, "Why is this?" You see, God made the world and the fullness thereof. Then He made man and gave man dominion over all the work of His hands (Gen. 1:28; Ps. 8:5,6). Adam was the "god" of this world. However, when Adam disobeyed God, he committed high treason and sold out his dominion on the earth to Satan. That's when Satan became the "god" of this world (2 Cor. 4:4).

God can't just move in on Satan's territory and take over. If He did, Satan could accuse Him of being unjust. However, God devised a plan of salvation and sent His Son, the Lord Jesus Christ, to consummate it.

Satan had no dominion over Jesus. Therefore, through Jesus, God could redeem mankind and restore to man his lost dominion over Satan. Now when we ask God to move on this earth, He can move in our behalf in Jesus' Name. That is why it seems He can do nothing unless someone asks Him to do it.

Even under the Old Covenant, people in covenant with God could pray and expect answers. For example, in Genesis 18, we find Abraham pleading his case to the Lord. Abraham's prayer here is one of the most illuminating prayers of the Old Testament. Abraham took his place in the covenant — what we call today the Old Covenant — that God had made with him.

GENESIS 18:23-25
23 And Abraham drew near, and said, Wilt thou also destroy the righteous with the wicked?

24 Peradventure there be fifty righteous within the city: wilt thou also destroy and not spare the place for the fifty righteous that are therein? 25 That be far from thee to do after this manner, to slay the righteous with the wicked: and that the righteous should be as the wicked, that be far from thee: SHALL NOT THE JUDGE OF ALL THE EARTH DO RIGHT?

In this account, we see that God did not destroy Sodom and Gomorrah until He had talked it over with Abraham, His blood-covenant friend. Through the covenant the Lord had just solemnized with Abraham, Abraham received rights and privileges about which most believers today have very little understanding.

That covenant gave Abraham legal standing with God. Therefore, according to the terms of that covenant, Abraham could speak plainly to the Lord as he interceded for Sodom and Gomorrah, saying, "Shall not the Judge of all the earth do right?"

Throughout the Old Testament we find people who not only understood their covenant rights but took their place in their covenant with God. For example, because Joshua took his place in the covenant, God parted the waters of the Jordan and caused the sun and moon to stand still in the heavens at Joshua's command (Joshua 3:10-17; 10:12-14).

Because Elijah took his place in the covenant, God sent fire out of Heaven to consume the altar as well as the sacrifice (1 Kings 18:31-38) and put the prophets of Baal to nought.

And when you read about David's mighty men in

the Old Testament, you would almost think you're read-ing about supermen; they were heroic warriors. David's mighty men of valor were utterly shielded from death in time of war as long as they remembered the covenant (2 Sam. 23:8-22).

Practically all the prayers of the Old Testament are prayers of covenant people praying to a faithful God who heard and answered prayer. Their prayers *had* to be answered. God *had* to give heed to the petitions of His people because of their *covenant* rights.

The believer today has covenant rights just as much as the Old Testament saints did. In fact, the Bible says we have a better covenant established upon better promises (Heb. 8:6). We ought to be able to do all they did and more because we have a new covenant, a better covenant, established upon greater promises.

Here is a challenge from a covenant-keeping God to Israel under the Old Covenant to plead their case with Him. How much more is it His challenge to the Church today!

> **ISAIAH 43:25,26**
> **25 I, even I, am he that blotteth out thy transgres-sions for mine own sake, and will not remember thy sins.**
> **26 Put me in remembrance: LET US PLEAD TOGETHER: declare thou, that thou mayest be justified.**

First, God said, "I am He who blots out your trans-gressions and I will not remember your sins." Thank God for that! If you are a child of God and have confessed your sins according to First John 1:9, then you have been cleansed of all unrighteousness by the blood of Jesus. God has no knowledge you ever did anything wrong.

Do you see what confidence that gives you? When you understand that fact, you can come to the Lord without a sense of sin-consciousness. You can come with faith and boldness and get your prayer heard and answered.

As long as a person comes to the Lord in prayer under condemnation and with a sense of spiritual inferiority, he will be tongue-tied and fear-filled in His Heavenly Father's Presence. And he will be hindered from receiving answers to his prayers. For instance, many times when people pray, they say, "I don't know if the Lord will hear me because I've missed it and failed. I'm such a failure!"

If you've confessed your sin to Him, God doesn't know you are a failure, so don't tell Him you are. He plainly said in Isaiah 43:25, "I will not remember your sins." He doesn't remember that you have done anything wrong, so why should you remind Him of it?

It isn't good taste to remind God of something you have already confessed to Him and been forgiven for. To remind Him that you did wrong in the past is to accuse Him of being a liar because He said you are cleansed from all unrighteousness (1 John 1:9).

God doesn't remember your past sins and failures — so don't you remember them either. Instead, come with confidence and boldness before the throne of grace, knowing that you have been made the righteousness of God by the precious blood of Jesus (Heb. 4:16; 2 Cor. 5:21).

Second, God said, *"PUT ME IN REMEMBRANCE: let us plead together: declare thou* [or set forth thy cause], *that thou mayest be justified"* (Isa. 43:26).

What does it mean to put God in remembrance? It means that as a covenant believer, you can stand before the throne of God when you pray and remind God of His promises. You can lay your case legally before Him and plead your case as a lawyer would plead his case before a judge. A lawyer is continually bringing up law and legal precedent. You bring God's Word to His attention: *"Put me in remembrance. . . ."* Put God in remembrance of His covenant promises: *". . . Shall not the Judge of all the earth do right?"* (Gen. 18:25).

In Isaiah 43:26, God is inviting you to put Him in remembrance of His Word. He is asking you to lay your case before Him and plead your covenant rights before Him using the legal precedence of His Word.

If you need healing, if your children are unsaved — *whatever* it is you are praying about — find Scripture that cover your case. Then lay the matter before your Heavenly Father.

How do you get God to move on your behalf? By standing on God's Word and pleading your case with Him. You find definite scriptures that promise what you need and continue to put God in remembrance of His Word according to your covenant rights. As you stand on God's Word and plead your case based on His promises, God will work on your behalf.

Isaiah 55:11 is an important scripture you should continually use in prayer as you stand on God's Word: *"So shall MY WORD be that goeth forth out of my mouth: it SHALL NOT RETURN UNTO ME VOID, but it shall accomplish that which I please, and it shall prosper in the thing whereto I sent it."*

This verse should be the very backbone of your prayer life. *No* word that has gone forth from God can return unto Him without accomplishing the purpose for which He sent it!

God said, *". . . I will hasten my word to perform it"* (Jer. 1:12). The marginal reading of the *King James Version* reads, "I will watch over My Word to perform it."

These scriptures are in perfect harmony with the following scripture from the New Testament.

JOHN 15:7
7 If ye abide in me, and my words abide in you, ye shall ask what ye will, and it shall be done unto you.

As a partner, a worker-together with God, you lay your case before Him. You call His attention to His part in your life. And because His Word abides in you, you can ask according to His Word and receive answers to your prayers.

God will make His Word good if you dare to stand by it! The greatest answers to prayer I have ever received occurred as a result of bringing God's Word to Him and reminding Him of what He said in His Word. Praise God, the Lord always keeps His Word!

Chapter 17
Redeemed From the Curse of Poverty

(Adapted originally from a RHEMA Bible Training Center classroom session with Kenneth Hagin.)

GALATIANS 3:13,14
13 CHRIST HATH REDEEMED US FROM THE CURSE OF THE LAW, being made a curse for us: for it is written, Cursed is every one that hangeth on a tree:
14 That the blessing of Abraham might come on the Gentiles through Jesus Christ; that we might receive the promise of the Spirit through faith.

Our text says, *"Christ hath REDEEMED us . . ."* (v. 13). If you ask Christians, even Spirit-filled Christians, "What did Christ redeem us from?" they usually say, "From sin." That's partly true, but not nearly all of the story.

The rest of verse 13 tells us in no uncertain terms what Christ redeemed us from: *"Christ hath redeemed us FROM THE CURSE OF THE LAW . . ."* (Gal. 3:13).

The expression "the Law" as used in the New Testament refers to either the Ten Commandments, the first five books of the Bible called the Pentateuch, or the whole of the Old Testament. In the Book of Deuteronomy, which is part of the Pentateuch, Moses stated the blessings and curses of the Law.

In the first part of Deuteronomy 28, God talks to Israel about the blessings of the Law that will overtake them if they obey His commands (vv. 1-14). Then skipping down to verse 15, God says, *"But it shall come to pass, if thou wilt NOT hearken unto the voice of the Lord thy God, to observe to do all his commandments and his statutes which I command thee this day; that ALL THESE CURSES shall come upon thee, and overtake thee."*

The curse or punishment for breaking God's commandments is threefold: *poverty, sickness,* and the *second death.* In this discussion, we'll only deal with the curse of poverty. Let's look at some verses that talk about the curse of poverty.

DEUTERONOMY 28:16-19,38-40
16 Cursed shalt thou be in the city, and cursed shalt thou be in the field.
17 Cursed shall be thy basket and thy store.
18 Cursed shall be the fruit of thy body, and the fruit of thy land, the increase of thy kine, and the flocks of thy sheep.
19 Cursed shalt thou be when thou comest in, and cursed shalt thou be when thou goest out. . . .
38 Thou shalt carry much seed out into the field, and shalt gather but little in; for the locust shall consume it.
39 Thou shalt plant vineyards, and dress them, but shalt neither drink of the wine, nor gather the grapes; for the worms shall eat them.
40 Thou shalt have olive trees throughout all thy coasts, but thou shalt not anoint thyself with the oil; for thine olive shall cast his fruit.

Poverty a Curse — *Not* a Blessing

You can readily see these verses are talking about poverty and lack. God said poverty and lack was a *curse* which was to come upon the people of God because they failed to keep His commandments and His statutes (Deut. 28:15).

The curse of poverty should come upon all of us — Gentiles and Jews alike — because all of us have sinned and come short of the glory of God (Rom. 3:23). But Galatians 3:13 tells us that instead of the curse coming upon us, Jesus was made to be a curse *for* us.

Jesus didn't go to the Cross for Himself — He did it for us! The curse fell on Him instead of upon us. He bore the curse for us so we wouldn't have to.

Jesus became our substitute and paid the debt for our sins through His death on the Cross. And God wrote it down as though we had paid the debt for sin ourselves! Now because of Jesus, we are free from the curse of the Law — and that includes the curse of poverty!

2 CORINTHIANS 8:9
9   For ye know the grace of our Lord Jesus Christ, that, though he was rich, yet for your sakes he became poor, that YE THROUGH HIS POVERTY MIGHT BE RICH.

Some endeavor to only put a spiritual interpretation on this verse. They say it's talking about Jesus becoming *spiritually* poor so we might be made *spiritually* rich. But there's more to this verse than that.

Although Jesus' needs were always supplied, if He became poor at all, it would only have been from the *material* standpoint because He never gathered to Himself earthly riches and treasures. For example, Jesus didn't even have His own home. He said about Himself, *". . . The foxes have holes, and the birds of the air have nests; but the Son of man hath not where to lay his head"* (Matt. 8:20).

But Jesus certainly wasn't spiritually poor. Someone who was spiritually poor could not work miracles, raise the dead, turn water into wine, feed five thousand with a little boy's lunch, or heal the sick!

Often people's thinking is out of line with the Bible, and that's what defeats them. They use some isolated scriptures to form an erroneous doctrine that is not in line with the whole counsel of God's Word.

For instance, some people have made a doctrine out of Luke 18:22, where Jesus tells the young rich man to *". . . sell all that thou hast, and distribute unto the poor, and thou shalt have treasure in heaven: and come, follow me."* These people try to use that verse to prove that *every* rich person who is born again needs to sell all his possessions and give to the poor.

Years ago down in the East Texas oilfields, I met a man who had been told that he had to sell everything he had in order to be saved. One night after I'd preached about our redemption from the curse of poverty, he said to me, "Brother Hagin, *now* I can be saved."

"What do you mean?" I asked.

He said, "Let me tell you my story. My wife and I were married as teenagers. We were brought up on the farm with no specialized training and very little education. All we knew was farming. So we saved enough money to make a down payment on ninety acres of farm land.

"The first and second year we were able to make our payments on our little farm. But the third year we had a crop failure, and we couldn't make the payments."

The bank gave this man and his wife grace that first year. But the next year they had another crop failure, and again they weren't able to make their payments. The bank was about to foreclose on them.

Just about that time, however, some people came along, wanting to lease this man's land to drill for oil. By leasing some of his land, he was able to pay off his farm.

This man's farm was one of the first farms in East Texas to be drilled for oil. Soon after these people began drilling for oil, they struck oil on this man's land. They put oil wells all over his farm, and he became very wealthy.

In the process of time, a church was started in that area where the Full Gospel message was preached, and this man's wife was saved and baptized in the Holy Spirit. He went to the meetings, too, but the minister told him that he'd have to sell everything he owned if he wanted to be saved. The minister based that on the story of the rich young ruler to whom Jesus said, "Sell all you have and give it to the poor" (Luke 18:22).

This man said to me, "I thought, *I can't do that! I*

*remember when we were in dire poverty and about to
lose everything we had. What would I do if I sold everything I own? I can't go back to farming."*

He continued, "I've come to this church regularly
now for twenty-five years. I've paid my tithes, given
offerings, supported missions, and helped send several
young people to Bible college. But in all that time, I've
never been born again. I just couldn't see how I could
sell everything I had and the preacher told me I had to
in order to be saved.

"But," he said, "after hearing you preach, Brother
Hagin, I realize I don't have to sell everything to get
saved. It's so good to know God doesn't want us to be
poor!"

Thank God, that man did get saved and baptized in
the Holy Spirit. But it's sad he went so long without
being born again. He could have been saved all along.

The minister at that man's church used an isolated
text which didn't mean what he thought it meant. He
thought Luke 18:22 meant you have to give everything
away to be saved. You don't.

Certainly if your material possessions are hindering
you from serving God with your whole heart, you need
to do something about that. But Jesus' words to the
young rich man are not a requirement for salvation!

It's not wrong to have money. It's wrong for money
to have *you!*

Another isolated text some people use to prove that
Christians aren't supposed to enjoy material prosperity

in this life is Mark 10:23: *". . . How hardly shall they that have riches enter into the kingdom of God!"* Some folks read that verse and say, "The Bible says a rich man can't get to Heaven."

But that's not what that verse says. That's the kind of wrong thinking that defeats people. We need to read the entire context of that verse to know what Jesus really meant. Jesus was saying we must put our trust in *God*, not in earthly riches. But He was *not* saying a rich man cannot be saved.

We cannot accept man's opinion. We have to take God's Word on the subject. Let the Word of God be the Supreme Court of appeal, the final say-so, on *any* subject.

The Word of God emphatically teaches that poverty is a curse (Deut. 28:16-19,38-40). And the Word of God teaches that Christ redeemed us from the curse of the Law, which includes the curse of poverty (Gal. 3:13). He redeemed us from poverty so we wouldn't have to live in poverty and lack in this life.

Let's look at what Jesus said during His earthly ministry about God meeting our material and financial needs.

MATTHEW 6:33
33 But seek ye first the kingdom of God, and his righteousness; and ALL THESE THINGS shall be added unto you.

Jesus is talking about the *material* things of life being added unto you, such as food to eat and clothes to

wear (Matt. 6:31,32). The way some people talk, it
sounds like Jesus said those things would be *taken
away* from you if you live for God.

> **LUKE 6:38**
> **38 GIVE, and IT SHALL BE GIVEN UNTO YOU;
> good measure, pressed down, and shaken
> together, and running over, shall men give into
> your bosom. For with the same measure that ye
> mete withal it shall be measured to you again.**

Did Jesus speak the truth when He made this
promise, or was He lying about it? I believe He told the
truth, don't you?

Notice Jesus said, ". . . *shall MEN give into your
bosom.* . . ." Of course, God is always the One who moti-
vates people to give to us as we believe and obey His
Word. However, God isn't going to rain down money
from Heaven to meet our needs! The money will come
from *people* on this earth.

Abraham's Blessing

In my own experience, I've found when I receive revelation about some scriptural truth and endeavor to
take a stand on it, there's always someone to argue,
"Yes, but that blessing is just for the Jews."

For instance, I've heard people argue, "Under the
Old Covenant, God promised to bless the Jews financially and materially, but that's not for us nowadays."

But did you ever study to find out who the Jews

really are? They were never called Jews until after the division of the tribes. The name "Jews" is a shortened version of the name, "Judah."

The blessing of the Old Covenant isn't the blessing of the tribe of *Judah.* The only blessing Judah received which was different from the other Israelite tribes was the promise that the Messiah would come from the tribe of Judah.

The blessing of the Old Covenant isn't the *Jews'* blessing; it's *Abraham's* blessing! Judah, as well as every other tribe of Israel, inherited the covenant promises through their father, Jacob, whose name was changed to Israel. Israel inherited the promise through his father, Isaac. Isaac inherited the promise through his father, Abraham. It's Abraham's blessing!

Now let's go back to Galatians 3 again: *"Christ hath redeemed us from the curse of the law, being made a curse for us: for it is written, Cursed is every one that hangeth on a tree: That THE BLESSING OF ABRA-HAM MIGHT COME ON THE GENTILES through Jesus Christ . . ."* (vv. 13,14).

Under the New Covenant, Abraham's blessing belongs to us! Christ has redeemed us from the curse of the Law so we wouldn't have to live under the curse — but under the *blessing.*

The blessing of Abraham is threefold in nature. It's a spiritual blessing, a physical blessing, and a material blessing. This agrees with what the Spirit of God said through the Apostle John in the New Testament.

3 JOHN 2
**2 Beloved, I wish above all things that thou
mayest PROSPER and BE IN HEALTH, even as
THY SOUL PROSPERETH.**

Let's go back once more to Deuteronomy. We've
looked at those scriptures which have to do with the
curse of poverty. Now let's look at the blessings of the
Law.

DEUTERONOMY 28:2
**2 And all these blessings shall come on thee, and
overtake thee, IF thou shalt HEARKEN unto the
voice of the Lord thy God.**

The truth is, the curse should come on us because
we've all sinned and come short of the glory of God
(Rom. 3:23). We've broken His commandments. But,
thank God, Christ redeemed us from the curse of the
Law, which we rightfully deserve. We were made righteous in Christ so that the blessing of Abraham could
come upon us (2 Cor. 5:21; Gal. 3:14)!

DEUTERONOMY 28:3-6,8
**3 Blessed shalt thou be in the city, and blessed
shalt thou be in the field.** [You'll be blessed wherever
you are!]
**4 Blessed shall be the fruit of thy body, and the
fruit of thy ground, and the fruit of thy cattle, the
increase of thy kine, and the flocks of thy sheep.
5 Blessed shall be thy basket and thy store.
6 Blessed shalt thou be when thou comest in, and
blessed shalt thou be when thou goest out. . . .**

8   The Lord shall command the blessing upon thee IN THY STOREHOUSES, and in all that thou settest thine hand unto; and he shall bless thee in the land which the Lord thy God giveth thee.

Some say you shouldn't desire material possessions in this life. But God says He will bless what you have *stored up*! He promises an abundant supply!

DEUTERONOMY 28:11-13
11   And the Lord shall make thee plenteous in goods, in the fruit of thy body, and in the fruit of thy cattle, and in the fruit of thy ground, in the land which the Lord sware unto thy fathers to give thee.
12   The Lord shall open unto thee his good treasure, the heaven to give the rain unto thy land in his season, and to bless all the work of thine hand: and thou shalt lend unto many nations, and THOU SHALT NOT BORROW.
13   And the Lord shall make thee the head, and not the tail; and thou shalt be above only, and thou shalt not be beneath. . . .

Verse 12 says, ". . . *thou shalt not borrow*." Does that mean it's wrong to borrow money? No. If it's wrong then God told the Israelites to do wrong when He told them to lend, and we know He wouldn't do that. Actually, God was saying, "I'm going to bless you so much you won't *have* to borrow."

You may not be at a place financially yet where you don't have to borrow. But begin to stand in faith for such an abundance that you don't have to borrow. It's a part of the blessing of Abraham that is yours in Christ!

The blessing of Abraham that has come upon us gives us a *full* supply — spiritually, physically, materially and financially.

PHILIPPIANS 4:19
19 But my God shall supply ALL your need ACCORDING TO HIS RICHES IN GLORY by Christ Jesus.

The phrase "all your need" would include financial and material needs, as well as spiritual needs. In fact, if you'll read the entire context, you'll find that Philippians 4:10-19 is specifically talking about financial and material needs.

There is an important balance to this subject of prosperity that people need to understand. God has promised to supply His children's every need. But that doesn't mean a person can just sit down and do nothing and expect God to bring the money in supernaturally. That's not in line with the whole counsel of the Word.

For example, the pastor of a church where I held a meeting once said to me, "Brother Hagin, I wish you'd talk to So-and-so," and he mentioned a certain fellow. "He has great confidence in you and your ministry, but he has misunderstood your teaching on prosperity.

"He was saved and baptized in the Holy Ghost at this church. But then he said he was going to believe God to supply all his needs, and he hasn't worked for nearly three years now.

"The church has had to help feed and clothe his three children. His wife is unskilled, so she's been taking in

ironing and doing housework for people in the church in
order to make ends meet. Meanwhile, this man sits at
home, believing that God is going to supply all his
needs!"

The pastor continued, "One of the board members in
the church offered this fellow a job. But the man said,
'No, I don't need a job. God has promised in His Word to
meet my needs. I'm living by faith.'"

That man wasn't living by faith! He was living in
ignorance! The same Bible which says God will supply
all our needs also says ". . . *if any would not work, nei-*
ther should he eat" (2 Thess. 3:10).

You do have a right to ask God to bless you financially just as He blessed Israel under the Old Covenant.
But God also promised to bless everything they set
their hands to: "I will bless the *work of your hands"*
(Deut. 28:12). God never promised to bless Israel if they
didn't set their hands to *something!*

God also said, *"Blessed shall be . . . the fruit of thy*
ground . . ." (Deut. 28:4). God couldn't bless the crops if
the Israelites hadn't planted them! And God promised
that His blessing would be upon their storehouses
(Deut. 28:8). But God wasn't going to fill the Israelites'
storehouses while they did nothing!

You see, you don't just sit down and do nothing and
say, "God is going to meet my needs." If you do, you'll
become a laughingstock to intelligent people, a
reproach to Christ, and a disgrace to the message of
faith. Put your hand to something and believe God to
prosper the work of your hands!

We can believe God and exercise faith for anything that is promised to us in the Bible. But we get on dangerous ground when we go beyond the Word. As long as you're in the Word, you're in the light! If you base what you believe on the Word, you're on safe ground!

So don't settle for living under the curse of poverty. You've been redeemed from that curse of the Law by the blood of Jesus Christ! Stand on God's Word and claim the blessing of Abraham that is yours in Christ. Believe God for a *full* supply in every area of your life!

Chapter 18
'Neither Give Place'

Neither give place to the devil.
— Ephesians 4:27

It is easy to leave the door open to the devil and not even intend to. Ephesians 4:27 says, *"Neither give place to the devil."* Paul didn't write that to sinners. He wrote that to Spirit-filled saints of God in the church at Ephesus. And what applies to the Christians in Ephesus applies to Christians today, wherever they might live.

Paul exhorted believers, "Don't give the devil any place in you." That means it's possible for you to give the devil place or an open door into your life. However, it also means that he can't take any place unless you *let* him!

You see, we have been delivered out of Satan's authority through Jesus' death and resurrection. He has absolutely *no* power over us unless we give him place in our lives.

> **COLOSSIANS 1:12-14**
> 12 Giving thanks unto the Father . . .
> 13 WHO HATH DELIVERED US FROM THE POWER OF DARKNESS, and hath translated us into the kingdom of his dear Son:
> 14 In whom we have redemption through his blood, even the forgiveness of sins.

Notice God has not promised to deliver us someday

in the future. Verse 13 and 14 says that by the blood of Jesus, God has *already* delivered us from the power of darkness.

That Greek word translated "power" means *authority*. So Colossians 1:13 is saying that God has delivered us out of Satan's *authority*.

This verse also says that God has "translated" us into the Kingdom of His dear Son. The word "translate" means *to take out of one and put into another*. We were taken *out of* Satan's family and placed *into* God's family. This happened legally when Jesus defeated Satan in His death, burial, and resurrection. Being delivered out of Satan's kingdom and placed into God's Kingdom became a reality in our individual lives when we were born again and made new creatures in Christ.

Our redemption is a present reality! We are not waiting for it to be manifested when we die and go to Heaven. Thank God, we have it *now* in *this* life! We are delivered *now* from the authority of darkness.

We are redeemed, and Satan has no more dominion over us. If we will just believe and act upon the authority Jesus gave us in His Name, we can enjoy the reality of that which is ours. And we can keep the door closed to the devil in our lives.

ROMANS 6:14
14 For SIN SHALL NOT HAVE DOMINION OVER YOU: for ye are not under the law, but under grace.

Another translation reads, "For sin shall not *lord* it over you. . . ." If anything has dominion over you, it is lording it over you.

In one sense, sin and Satan are synonymous terms. The Bible says sin shall not lord it over you. And as we've seen from the Word, Satan has no legal authority over you either. Why not? Because you have a new Lord, the Lord Jesus Christ. Thank God, Jesus is your Lord — not Satan!

Satan shall not lord it over you. Satan has no more dominion over you, the believer, than Pharaoh had over the children of Israel after they crossed the Red Sea. When Pharaoh's hosts attempted to cross the Red Sea to recapture the Israelites, the parted waters rushed in upon them and they were drowned in the depths of the sea (Exod. 14:28-30).

Israel was forever free from Pharaoh; he had no more dominion over them. In the same way, Satan has no more authority or dominion over believers.

You are forever delivered from Satan's kingdom of darkness. He was conquered and defeated by Jesus at the Cross! Jesus did it for you. His victory is *your* victory because you are *in Him!*

There is no need for you to be defeated by the devil. He is a defeated foe! The Bible says to resist the devil and he will flee from you (James 4:7). It doesn't say he *might* flee from you — it says he *will* flee from you. He will flee from *you* when you stand in the authority of Jesus' Name.

However, along with our authority in the Name of Jesus to resist Satan, comes our responsibility to always keep the door closed to the devil. The devil has no authority over us *unless we give him place.*

Some believers have thought, *I'm born again and blood-bought, so I'm automatically safe from the attacks of the devil.*

We *are* protected *if* we believe and obey God's Word. But if we were automatically safe from the onslaughts of the enemy with no responsibility on our part, why would Paul have given us the admonition: *"Neither give place to the devil"?*

It would have been foolish for Paul to make a statement like that if it was impossible for the devil to get into our lives no matter *what* we do.

No, God said through Paul, "Don't give the devil any place in you." That means the devil *can* take a place in you — if you *let* him.

We are not to let sin have dominion over us. Sin opens the door to the devil in our lives. And that doesn't just mean "big" sins, like robbery or murder. Any kind of disobedience to God's Word gives the devil a place in our lives.

A lot of times we make the mistake of trying to catalog sins. We put one at the top of our list and say, "That sin is terrible." And we put another sin down at the bottom of the list and say, "That one isn't too bad."

But God doesn't categorize sins the same way many believers would. Look in the Book of Revelation to see *God's* perspective of sin.

REVELATION 21:8
8   But the FEARFUL, and UNBELIEVING, and

the ABOMINABLE, and MURDERERS, and WHORE-
MONGERS, and SORCERERS, and IDOLATERS,
and all LIARS, shall have their part in the lake
which burneth with fire and brimstone: which is
the second death.

God begins his list with the *fearful*. How many of us
would put fear first in a list of terrible sins?

Then God lists the *unbelieving*. Did you know we
have a lot of unbelieving believers? God mentioned the
unbelieving before He ever listed the murderers and
the whoremongers. We would probably change the
order of those sins around, but God doesn't look at
things the way we do.

Let's talk about fear for a moment. Fear is one of
the main strategies Satan uses to defeat believers. Fear
is of the enemy, not of God.

Second Timothy 1:7 says, *"For God hath not given
us THE SPIRIT OF FEAR; but of power, and of love,
and of a sound mind."* Notice this verse calls fear a
spirit. The Spirit of power, love, and a sound mind is
the Holy Ghost.

In my experience of praying for folks, I can safely
say that eighty-five percent of them are influenced by a
spirit of fear. A spirit of fear is one of the most predomi-
nant attacks of the enemy we face today. We are living
in an age of fear.

Believers need to be careful not to give place to the
spirit of fear. Some have opened the door to the devil
through fear, which allows other spirits to get in and
harass them.

The Bible teaches that giving an evil spirit any inroad into our lives opens the door to other evil spirits.

MATTHEW 12:43-45
43 When the unclean spirit is gone out of a man, he walketh through dry places, seeking rest, and findeth none.
44 Then he saith, I will return into my house from whence I came out; and when he is come, he findeth it empty, swept, and garnished.
45 Then goeth he, and TAKETH WITH HIMSELF SEVEN OTHER SPIRITS more wicked than himself, and THEY ENTER IN and DWELL THERE: and the last state of that man is worse than the first. . . .

Opening the door to the spirit of fear is one way we can give other spirits the opportunity to come in and wreak havoc in our lives.

For example, in the case of Job, we can see the danger of allowing fear to have dominion over us. Job lost his children, his property, and his health through Satan's attacks (Job 1:13-19). How was Satan able to attack Job? Satan had to have some avenue, some inroad into Job's life.

The Bible says that Job was in fear. After all these calamities came upon him, Job said, *"For the thing which I GREATLY FEARED IS COME UPON ME, and THAT WHICH I WAS AFRAID OF is come unto me"* (Job 3:25).

People sometimes say, "Satan was able to attack Job because God gave Satan permission." No, God didn't permit Satan to attack Job in the sense of *commissioning* the devil. *Job* gave Satan permission by opening the door to him through fear. God only allowed Satan to do what Job had already permitted through the open door of fear.

Fear opens the door to the enemy. Fear is not of God! You see, legally Satan is the god of this world (2 Cor. 4:4). We are living in this world where Satan is god. Satan has a right to take a place in our lives if we get on his territory and *give* place to him through sin and disobedience. And one way to give place to the devil is by allowing the spirit of fear to influence us.

How do you keep fear out of your life? When the devil tries to bring thoughts of fear into your mind, resist those thoughts with the authority God has given you in the Name of Jesus.

Command fear to *go* in Jesus' Name! Then fill your mind instead with the promises in God's Word, and confess those promises with your mouth. When you act upon the Word and use your authority to resist the devil in the Name of Jesus, fear *has* to go. Remember, you have *not* been given a spirit of fear, but of power, love, and a sound mind (2 Tim. 1:7)!

You can open the door to the devil by allowing any sin to have dominion over you. For example, you can open the door to the devil through *unforgiveness* and *resentment*. It can be a real temptation to harbor resentment toward someone you feel has wronged you. It's easy to think, *I'm just not ready to forgive that person yet.* But often the truth of the matter is you just want to hold on to the resentment and make the person pay for the wrong he or she did to you!

When you don't immediately forgive a person who has wronged you, you open the door to the devil. Strife and unforgiveness open the door to confusion, ill health, poverty, and every evil work (James 3:16). So get rid of unforgiveness and resentment just as quickly as you can! The Bible says, "*A merry heart doeth good like a medicine . . .*" (Prov. 17:22). Your heart is your spirit. A resentful and unforgiving heart is not merry.

A merry heart has a life-giving effect on you; it works on you like medicine. On the negative side, the opposite is true. An unforgiving, revengeful heart or a doubting, fearful heart open the door to the devil and can make you sick or depressed.

The devil tries to get you to give him place in your life through any sin, including fear, unbelief, and unforgiveness. But you *never* have to give him place. You have been delivered from *all* the power of darkness (Col. 1:13).

So learn to resist Satan. Put the devil in his place! Say, "Fear, I resist you in the Name of Jesus. I *refuse* to fear. Doubt, I resist you in the Name of Jesus. I *refuse* to doubt." And determine in your heart to always walk in love and to *immediately* forgive whoever might offend you. That's how you keep the door closed to the devil in your life.

You can do it! You can do *all* things through Christ who strengthens you (Phil. 4:13). If you can't, then God lied about it when He said through Paul, "Don't you give *any* place to the devil."

You have the authority over the devil because Jesus

gave you that authority. He said, ". . . *All power* [authority] *is given unto me in heaven and in earth"* (Matt. 28:18). Then He immediately delegated that authority on the earth to believers when He said, *"Go YE therefore . . ."* (Matt. 28:19). In the mighty Name of Jesus, we have authority over all the power of the enemy (Luke 10:19)!

Once you get a revelation of the authority that is yours in Jesus' Name, you won't run from the devil any longer — you'll put *him* on the run! Instead of your being afraid of him, *he'll* be afraid of *you* because you know the truth about who you are in Christ. You know you can keep the door closed to the devil and be strong in the power of Jesus Christ.

Our ability to live free from the power of the enemy is all a part of God's plan of redemption through Jesus Christ. We weren't delivered from the power of darkness because of anything *we* did, but because of what *Jesus* did for us.

Jesus rose victorious over death, hell, and the grave. God raised Him from the dead, and gave Him a Name above every name. And that Name belongs to you and me.

Because of Jesus, we have the authority to say to the devil: "In Jesus' Name I resist you! In Jesus' Name I stand against every strategy you have arrayed against me! You have *no* authority over me, for through Jesus I have been delivered from the power of darkness. And, Satan, for the rest of my life, I *refuse* to give you *any* place in me!"

A Spiritual Psalm

Trials do not come from Heaven;
Tests do not come from God.
Yea, the enemy as you trod the pathway down here,
Will put pressure on you from every side.
Darkness does not come from Heaven;
There is no darkness there.
All is light!
But the darkness of life, the trials of life,
Come because the enemy stirs up strife.
He would rob you of faith;
He would cause you to doubt.
Yea, he would afflict your body,
And cause you to lose your shout.
He would move in your life to cause you to be afraid.
He would fill you with fear and depression as you walk
    down here.
But *the Lord* in His mercy,
Doth minister to His own!
Yea, His eye is on the sparrow;
And He has not forsaken you!
Even in the midst of darkness,
In the midst of the night,
In the midst of the storm,
He will cause thee to be at rest and filled with peace,
So that in your life there is no fright.
Even in the midst of the storm,
When the winds of adversity blow,
Yea, you can look the enemy in the face,
And fill your heart and spirit and mouth
With laughter that is of a holy glee!
Because, you see, the Greater One in you doth dwell!
He will rise up in you and give illumination unto your mind;

Direction unto your spirit
So ye shall not need to question
And wonder "Why?"
But you shall *know*
That the Lord is on your side!
He'll see you through.
He'll lift you up and establish your goings
So you can rejoice in the midst of adversity;
You can rejoice in the midst of trial;
You can rejoice in the midst of test;
And you can praise the Lord all the while!
A spirit of resentment,
A spirit of revenge in the heart of the believer
Will open the door for Satan to come in.
He will strike you in the nighttime
When you are asleep upon your pillow
Because you left the door open,
And ofttime afflict you in mind and in body
Because you entertained a spirit of revenge —
A spirit that was not right.
And so the door was left open.
An unforgiving spirit will leave the door ajar.
And surely the enemy walketh about as a roaring lion,
Seeking whom he may devour.
If the door is open, the devil can come in.
But *if the door is closed,* he cannot enter in.
Shut the door on him even now!
Let not a spirit of resentment in your life abide.
Let not a spirit of revenge about you reside.
Let not an unforgiving spirit draw nigh unto thee.
But freely forgive,
For you have been freely forgiven!

You will find that you can walk
In spiritual health, mental health, and physical health.
But open the door to the enemy,
And surely you shall defeated be.
Close the door!
Let your mind be stayed on Him!
Freely forgive from your heart
Your neighbor, your friend,
your brother, your sister, your family.
Yea, let no resentment build up within.
Let no spirit of revenge reside,
Or that quick forked tongue
That would strike to cut and hurt.
Let that tongue be sanctified.
Let your words be seasoned with grace
And soaked in love.
Be swift to hear, slow to speak, and slow to wrath
As you walk down here.
And if you will, you will find
That life will better be;
You will find that you will walk
In a greater degree of spirituality.
You will find that the blessings of the Lord
Upon you shall reside;
And the enemy, when you resist him,
Will run away and hide!

Chapter 19
Where Sickness Comes From

> *Jesus saith unto him, Have I been so long time with you, and yet hast thou not known me, Philip? HE THAT HATH SEEN ME HATH SEEN THE FATHER; and how sayest thou then, Shew us the Father?*
>
> — John 14:9

> *How God anointed Jesus of Nazareth with the Holy Ghost and with power: who went about doing GOOD, and HEALING all that were OPPRESSED of the DEVIL; for God was with him.*
>
> — Acts 10:38

As long as you think sickness is a blessing from Heaven, you'll entertain it, receive it, clasp it to your bosom, and own it. You need to know beyond a shadow of a doubt that sickness and disease do *not* come from God.

The Bible says, *"Every good gift and every perfect gift is from above, and cometh down from the Father of lights . . ."* (James 1:17). Sickness can't be a gift that God sends down from Heaven because there isn't any sickness or disease in Heaven.

Also, sickness can't be a "good and perfect gift." The Bible says in Acts 10:38 that God anointed Jesus of Nazareth who went about doing *good* — and making

199

people sick? No! He went about doing good and *healing* all who were sick and oppressed of the *devil*!

People who are unacquainted with the Word often don't realize that ever since the fall of man, there has been a curse on the earth. And because people don't understand that they live in a fallen world where Satan dominates, they accuse God of causing accidents that take place. They accuse God of causing sickness and the death of loved ones. They accuse God of causing storms, earthquakes, and floods. Even insurance policies call such catastrophes "acts of God."

But we know sickness, disease, accidents, and natural catastrophes cannot be from God because they are certainly not good and perfect gifts. No, Satan is the god of this world (2 Cor. 4:4). And John 10:10 says, *"The THIEF* [Satan] *cometh not, but for to STEAL, and to KILL, and to DESTROY. . . ."* Anything that steals, kills, and destroys is from the devil. Therefore, the bad things that happen on this earth come from Satan; they're not acts of God!

A look at Jesus' ministry also proves that sickness, disease, and natural catastrophes don't come from God. Jesus was and is God's will in action.

In John 14:10 Jesus said to His disciples, *". . . the words that I speak unto you I speak not of myself: but the Father that dwelleth in me, HE DOETH THE WORKS."* If you want to see the works of God, look at Jesus! If you want to hear the words of God, listen to Jesus!

Another time Jesus said, *". . . I came down from heaven, not to do mine own will, but the will of him that sent me"* (John 6:38). When Jesus was on this earth, He never did anything outside of the will of God. So we can look at Jesus to find out what God's will is.

For instance, once Jesus and His disciples were crossing the Sea of Galilee and a violent storm arose (Mark 4:36-39). The fearful disciples awakened Jesus, crying, ". . . *Master, carest thou not that we perish?"* (Mark 4:38).

What was God's will in the situation? To find out, we have to look to Jesus. The Bible says Jesus rebuked the wind and the waves, saying, "Peace, be still!" (Mark 4:39).

When Jesus rebuked the storm, He wasn't rebuking something *God* was doing. He was doing the will of His Heavenly Father by halting the work of the devil.

John Alexander Dowie was a nineteenth-century Congregationalist minister who received light on divine healing, the power of God, and faith. I once read where Dowie said, "I've crossed the ocean fourteen times, and every time, storms have arisen. Each time without exception I stood on the deck of the ship and commanded the storm, 'In Jesus' Name, peace, be still!' Each time the storm ceased."

Dowie recognized that God didn't cause the storm. He knew the destructive forces of nature came into existence when Satan became the god of this world.

We can also look at Jesus to see what God's will is concerning sickness and disease. Not once in Jesus' ministry did He turn anyone down who came to Him for healing.

Once a leper came to Jesus and said, ". . . *Lord, if thou wilt, thou canst make me clean*" (Matt. 8:2). Jesus *didn't* say, "Now, my son, God moves in mysterious ways, His wonders to perform. His ways are past finding out. Man in his small finite mind can never understand the infinite. God has some purpose in your affliction. Just be patient and let patience have her perfect work."

Jesus *didn't* say, "You see, God loves you so much He brought this disease on you to deepen your piety and teach you a good spiritual lesson. So learn your lesson well and maybe eventually God will heal you — *if* it's His will."

No! Jesus *never* said anything like that. And no man has a right to speak that kind of religious tradition in His Name!

When the leper asked Jesus to heal him, Jesus simply said, "I will." Praise God, that statement settles forever the matter of whether or not it is God's will to heal!

Jesus is God's will in action. Jesus never did *anything* outside the will of God. So when He healed the leper, He was doing God's will.

In the account where Jesus healed the woman who was bowed over with the spirit of infirmity, Jesus said, ". . . *ought not this woman, being a daughter of Abraham, WHOM SATAN HATH BOUND, lo, these eighteen years, be loosed from this bond on the sabbath day?*" (Luke 13:16).

Who did Jesus say bound that woman? He said *Satan* did.

Remember in our text Jesus said, "He that has seen *Me* has seen the *Father*" (John 14:9). As I study the healing ministry of Jesus, that statement makes it impossible for me to accept the teaching that disease and sickness come from our Father God.

Jesus' commission to believers just before He ascended to Heaven also proves that healing comes from God, not sickness. In Mark 16:15 Jesus said, *". . . Go ye into all the world, and preach the gospel to every creature."* Then Jesus said, *"And these signs shall follow them that believe. . . ."* (Mark 16:17). One of the signs Jesus gave was that believers would *". . . lay hands on the SICK, and they SHALL RECOVER"* (Mark 16:18).

Jesus sent the Church into the world to minister as He had ministered — preaching the gospel *and* healing the sick. In that Great Commission, Jesus was expressing the Father's will. God doesn't *send* sickness and disease *on* people. He wants to *set them free* from sickness and disease.

When people try to figure out where sickness and disease come from, they often get confused because they haven't taken time to get into the Word for themselves. Instead of studying to see what the Word of God has to say on the subject, they've just accepted what some unbelieving minister said about it or what their church taught about it.

As a young Baptist boy, I was ignorant about this subject myself. All I knew was that I'd been sick all my life; that I had a deformed heart; and that I had never

run and played like other children. All I knew was that
I had been bedfast for sixteen months, and that five
doctors had told me I would die.

Then I received the revelation of Mark 11:24:
". . . *What things soever ye desire, when ye pray, believe
that ye receive them, and ye shall have them.*" I came to
understand that the prayer of faith works. Through the
prayer of faith, I was healed from paralysis and an
incurable blood disease and raised up from a deathbed.

But I had only received one little glimpse of light
regarding divine healing. I still didn't know where sickness comes from.

I didn't know yet that healing was in the atonement
(Isa. 53:4,5). I didn't know Jesus bore our sicknesses
(Matt. 8:17). I didn't know that by Jesus' stripes, we
were healed (1 Peter 2:24). I didn't know Satan was the
author of sickness and disease. So the fear of becoming
sick again continued to torment me.

Certainly I believed in divine healing. As a young
Baptist pastor, I laid hands on the sick, anointed them
with oil, and saw them healed. And after I was baptized
with the Holy Ghost and began pastoring a Full Gospel
church, I continued to pray for the sick with good
results. But I was still ignorant about where sickness
comes from. Satan took advantage of my ignorance and
hounded me with the fear that I might someday become
bedfast or paralyzed again.

That fear followed me everywhere I went. It wasn't
in me. It was somewhere on the *outside* of me, pursuing
me like an annoying dog that tags along behind. The

Bible says fear is a spirit (2 Tim. 1:7).

The fear would catch up to me every now and then. I would endeavor to resist and rebuke it. When I did that, it seemed to stand off a few feet away from me, but it would never leave me for good.

Then one night I read a book written by a medical doctor named Dr. Lilian B. Yeomans. One chapter in that book discussed sickness as a *curse*, not a blessing. In that chapter, Dr. Yeomans asked the question, "Where does sickness come from?" She stressed the importance of finding the *source* of any problem, including sickness, in order to find a solution to the problem. She related an incident that happened in her own life as an illustration.

During World War I, Dr. Yeomans left an active healing ministry to offer her assistance as a medical doctor to the United States government. When a typhoid epidemic struck in a small mountain community, the government sent in a company of doctors, headed by Dr. Yeomans, to keep the typhoid from spreading.

The doctors knew they could only stop the epidemic if they found the source of the problem. So they asked the residents, "Where is the source of your water?"

The people told the doctors that the water source for the entire community was further up in the mountains where the people had dug out a cistern. Winter snows and spring rains filled the cistern with water. Then the water flowed down the mountains through a pipe to the village.

When the doctors checked the cistern, they found out that an old sow and ten pigs had fallen into it. The dead pigs had contaminated the water. So the doctors cleaned out the cistern and the typhoid epidemic was stopped — not by medical science, but just by *finding the source of the problem.*

After relating this incident, Dr. Yeomans proposed that finding out that sickness and disease comes from the devil will help us put a stop to sickness and disease in our lives.

Dr. Yeomans explained that sickness doesn't come from Heaven because there isn't any sickness there. And it doesn't come from God. When God made man, He didn't make him sick. God saw that the work of His hands was *good* (Gen. 1:31).

God is not the author of sickness. Man never became sick until *after* he listened to the devil.

You see, God told Adam, "I give you dominion over all the work of my hands" (Gen. 1:28-30). In other words, God said, "I'm turning the earth over to you, Adam."

Adam had the legal right, although not the *moral* right, to give the dominion over the earth to the devil. And that's exactly what Adam did. When Adam disobeyed God, he committed high treason and the devil then became the god of this world (2 Cor 4:4). Only then did man fall heir to sickness and disease.

As I read this chapter in Dr. Yeoman's book, I finally saw it. I saw that sickness was a curse. I saw that it came from hell, *not* Heaven. I saw that it came from

Satan, *not* God.

I was so thrilled, I couldn't stay in bed. Even though I'm conservative by nature, I jumped out of bed and had a running spell. I ran around and around that room in my bare feet, rejoicing in the Lord! Glory to God, I *couldn't* be still! I had just discovered where sickness comes from, and I *knew* I never had to be sick again. Anything that was of the devil was something I *refused* to accept!

When I got this revelation from God's Word, it dispelled the fear that had hounded me for some time. The fear of getting sick again had continually dogged my tracks, taking advantage of what I didn't know. That fear was gone forever!

That demon of fear said, "Oh, no, he found out the truth!" And he finally left me for good. Oh, it's so wonderful to be free!

Sickness and disease are of the devil. Let the truth of that statement sink deep in your spirit. Then follow in the footsteps of Jesus and deal with sickness the way Jesus did. Treat sickness and disease as an enemy and never tolerate it in your life.

In His earthly ministry, Jesus continually healed the sick and broke Satan's dominion over the lives of men and women. You have the authority to do the same in the Name of Jesus. Claim the Father's good and perfect gift of *healing* for yourself and others, and walk in the fullness of the salvation Jesus provided for you!

Chapter 20
The Truth Shall Set You Free

. . . the yoke shall be destroyed because of the
anointing.

— Isaiah 10:27

And ye shall know the truth, and the truth
shall make you free.

— John 8:32

It's the anointing or power of the Holy Spirit that
breaks the yoke of bondage. The yoke can be anything
that binds you. It can be sickness or disease, bad
habits, or demonic activity. But the yoke of bondage
shall be destroyed because of the anointing!

The anointing of the Holy Spirit is on God's Word.
John 8:32 says that the truth — God's Word — shall set
you free. You might say, "But I thought it was the
anointing that breaks the yoke." That's right, but Jesus
said His words are *spirit* and *life* (John 6:63). The Word
of God is anointed by the Spirit of God. That's the reason the truth of the Word will set you free.

Jesus made this request of His Father in John
17:17: *"Sanctify them through thy truth: THY WORD IS*
TRUTH." So the Word and truth are interchangeable
terms. This means we could read John 8:32: "You shall
know the *Word*, and the *Word* shall make you free."

I feel sorry for Christians who don't know the Word. You see them throughout the Body of Christ — bound up, failing, and stumbling by the wayside. God said, *"My people are destroyed for lack of knowledge . . ."* (Hosea 4:6). Here's another way to say it: "God's people are destroyed for lack of knowledge of the truth of His Word."

But when people possess the knowledge of the truth in God's Word, they won't be destroyed any longer. Thank God for the Word! Thank God for the truth that sets us free!

In 1939, my wife and I accepted the pastorate of a church in north Texas. I had been among Pentecostal people for about two years. I had seen other Pentecostal pastors conduct every kind of service you could think of, so I followed their example.

I started having a deliverance service every Saturday night. We prayed for the people to get delivered. We laid hands on them and anointed them with oil. And during those services we had just about every kind of manifestation imaginable.

The deliverance services seemed to go well for a while. But after about three months, the crowd began to wane. Deliverance began to get old to them, so I decided to change the name of our Saturday night services to "getting free" services. Now everyone who had gotten *delivered* in the last ninety days came to get *free*!

The getting free services seemed to go well for a while. Then the novelty began to wear off. I decided we needed to do something else, so I announced that we were going to start having "loosening" services every Saturday night. And I noticed that the same people who had come for three months to get *delivered* and for three more months to get *free*, now came to get *loosened!*

Our loosening services lasted for about ninety days too. By then I began to realize that something was wrong. We had been having deliverance, getting free, and loosening meetings for nine months. During those services, we had people shout and jump because they were so thrilled. We had every kind of manifestation imaginable! Yet I could see that the people weren't any more delivered, free, or loosened than they were when we started!

I said to myself, *As the pastor, I visit and talk to these people every day, and I can see they're not free. They shout at church, but at home they're just as bound as they were before. If that's all it means to be delivered, loosened, or set free, these meetings aren't worth anything.* So I began to fast and pray and seek the Lord about it.

On the third day of my fast, the Lord spoke to me. He said, "You are trying to obtain through prayer, laying on of hands, anointing with oil, and shouting and praising, what only *My Word* will bring."

You see, all our praying, shouting, and jumping — or whatever we're doing — needs to be in line with God's Word, because God has magnified His Word above His Name (Ps. 138:2). If we're not careful, we can substitute a lot of things that may seem good and legitimate for the Word of God.

During that fast, the Lord gave me John 8:32: *"And
ye shall know the truth, and the truth shall make you
free."* Jesus said to me, "People might receive temporary
help and get blessed momentarily because they are
honest and they're seeking Me. But the only thing that
will permanently bless people is *to know the truth of
My Word."*

The Word is anointed by the Holy Spirit. And when
you know God's Word, that anointed Word will *permanently* bless you by setting you free!

So I began to do what God showed me. I began to
teach and preach more of the Word. And just as the Lord
promised me, my congregation began to be set free.

And the people stayed free! Years afterwards, when
I was out in the field ministry, I saw some of those same
people. They told me, "Brother Hagin, we're still living
on what you taught us about the Word when you were
our pastor."

God's Word is truth, and knowledge of His Word
sets us free. No matter what the circumstances are, no
matter what you face in life, train yourself to always
ask the question, "What does the Word say about it?" In
other words, *put the Word first!*

If you don't know the Word, then you are in trouble.
You'll remain in bondage, for it is knowledge of the
Word that makes you free.

Our problem so much of the time is we are looking
for someone else to make us free. Instead of looking to
the Word and trusting in Jesus, we look to man and
trust in man. But we should be looking to *Jesus.*

Jesus has already won the victory! The Word of God
tells us that deliverance from *all* the power of the
enemy already belongs to us through Christ (Luke
10:19; Col. 1:13).

Through the Holy Spirit, God has given us the Bible
so that knowledge of what He has done for us can set us
free. For example, to set us free from sickness and disease, the Bible tells us, ". . . *Himself took our infirmities, and bare our sicknesses*" (Matt. 8:17), and ". . . *by
whose stripes ye were healed*" (1 Peter 2:24).

When it comes to the truth of healing, people miss it
many times by substituting what God's Word says with
their own thinking. That's why they're not free from
sickness and disease.

What we need to do is simply look to the Word of
God and do what the Word says. Agree with it. Side in
with the Word, not against it. It is only knowledge of
the anointed Word that will set us free.

For example, let's look at a healing in the ministry
of Jesus because that shows how *knowing* and *acting* on
the Word sets people free from sickness and disease.

Jesus ministered under the anointing of the Holy
Spirit. He said, "*The Spirit of the Lord is upon me,
because HE HATH ANOINTED ME . . .*" (Luke 4:18).
His words were also anointed, for He said, ". . . *the
words that I speak unto you, they are SPIRIT, and they
are LIFE*" (John 6:63). Remember, it's the anointing
that breaks the yoke.

JOHN 4:46-53
**46 So Jesus came again into Cana of Galilee,
where he made the water wine. And there was a**

certain nobleman, whose son was sick at Caper-
naum.
47 When he heard that Jesus was come out of
Judaea into Galilee, he went unto him, and
besought him that he would come down, and heal
his son: for he was at the point of death.
48 Then said Jesus unto him, Except ye see signs
and wonders, ye will not believe.
49 The nobleman saith unto him, Sir, come down
ere my child die.
50 Jesus saith unto him, GO THY WAY; THY SON
LIVETH. And the man BELIEVED the WORD that
Jesus had spoken unto him, and he WENT HIS
WAY.
51 And as he was now going down, his servants
met him, and told him, saying, Thy son liveth.
52 Then enquired he of them the hour when he
began to amend. And they said unto him, Yesterday at the seventh hour the fever left him.
53 So the father knew that it was at the same
hour, in the which Jesus said unto him, Thy son
liveth: and himself believed, and his whole house.

Notice the Bible says that when Jesus said, "Go
your way; your son lives," the man ". . . *BELIEVED the*
WORD that Jesus had spoken unto him, and HE
WENT HIS WAY" (John 4:50). The nobleman went his
way even though he had no evidence of his son's healing
other than Jesus' Word.

The nobleman had no physical evidence of his son's
healing until his servants told him, ". . . *Thy son*
liveth . . ." (v. 51). When the nobleman asked them what
hour his son began to amend or get well, they
answered, ". . . *Yesterday at the seventh hour* . . ." (v. 52).

I want you to see several important things here.

First, this man demonstrated that he believed the Word that Jesus spoke to him, because he did what Jesus told him to do — he went his way. *Faith is acting on one's knowledge of God's Word.*

Second, notice that the son's healing began to take place *from the time Jesus spoke the Word.* The fever broke immediately, but the Bible says he *began* to amend from that hour. He continued to convalesce and become well; He wasn't healed instantly.

That's where a lot of people miss it when it comes to healing. If they're not immediately healed one hundred percent, they say, "I didn't get anything."

Yet the healing of this nobleman's son was not instantaneous. And it took place under the ministry of Jesus Christ, the Son of God! The Bible says Jesus had the Spirit of God without measure (John 3:34), yet this man's son was not instantly healed. The boy *began* to amend in the same hour Jesus said to the nobleman, "*. . . Thy son liveth . . .*" (John 4:53).

Many people turn the switch of faith off if there is not an instant, total manifestation of healing. But you need to *know the truth* about healing. The Word of God teaches us that a healing which takes place over a period of time is *also* miraculous because it says the healing of the nobleman's son was the second *miracle* Jesus did in Cana of Galilee (John 4:54).

I remember after I was healed, I didn't look any different than I did before I was healed. I weighed just eighty-nine pounds. And, naturally, I was terribly weak because I had been bedfast for sixteen long months.

My heart seemed to beat normally. But if I exerted myself even a little bit, it would start pounding. I didn't even have to put my hand up to my chest to feel it pounding. I was just a skeleton with a little skin stretched over the bones. I didn't *look* healed. But, thank God, I began to amend from that hour. And that was a miracle!

Keep the switch of faith turned on. I've been saying this for a good many years, but I'm more convinced today than ever: Every single time hands are laid on you in faith by *any* believer, healing begins right then!

So many times healing is never consummated because people turn the switch of faith off. In the same way that turning a light switch on causes the power of electricity to flow and light a room, the switch of faith keeps the power of God flowing. Turn off the switch and the power stops flowing.

What do I mean when I say, "Keep the switch of faith turned on"? Learn what the Word promises you and then believe and act upon your knowledge of the truth. Don't give up just because in the natural it looks like your faith isn't working.

This nobleman believed the Word Jesus had spoken and went his way. Go your way believing that what God has spoken in His Word is true. Continue to act upon your knowledge of the Word in faith and it will become a reality in your life. Remember, you'll know the truth, and the truth will make you free!

People see the sick being healed instantly when the healing anointing is in manifestation, and they think it ought to work that way with everyone, every time. But it didn't work that way with the nobleman's son, did it? From that hour he *began* to amend. We need to be ready and willing to follow God's leading, *whatever* He wants us to do.

If you say, "But I want God to do it my way," you are setting yourself up for a downfall. Doing things *our* way only keeps us in bondage. It's the knowledge of *God's* truth that sets us free.

Thank God for His Word! Remember, the only thing that will permanently bless people is to know the truth of God's Word.

When you *know* God's Word and *act* upon it, you won't need to look to man to set you free. That anointed Word will break every yoke of bondage and set you free, no matter *what* your need is.

So put God's Word first in your life. No matter what comes in life, train yourself to ask, "What does God's Word say about it?" Then act upon the knowledge of that truth and watch it set you free!

Chapter 21
Our Words Dominate Our Lives

But without faith it is impossible to please him: for he that cometh to God must believe that he is, and that he is a rewarder of them that diligently seek him.

— Hebrews 11:6

I'm convinced that few Christians realize this important fact: Our words dominate us. We will never rise above the confession of our lips. We will either rise or fall to the level of our confession.

Many times people discover the power of their words and make it work for them, even though they are not saved. For instance, someone might continually tell himself, *I can do anything I put my mind to.* As he says that with his mouth and believes it in his heart, he will become successful at what he puts his hand to. He might not understand the spiritual law behind what he's doing, but it will work for him anyway.

On the other hand, I have heard people look at a task set before them and say, "I can't do it." The moment they said that, they were defeated.

The moment you say you do not have faith, doubt will rise up like a giant and bind you. You are *imprisoned* by your negative words. Proverbs 6:2 says, *"Thou art snared with the words of thy mouth. . . ."* The margin of the *King James Version* says, "Thou art taken captive with the words of thy mouth." In other words, whether good or bad, *your words dominate you.*

Our confession is a vital part of our faith. And Hebrews 11:6 tells us that God demands that we have faith in order to please Him. If God demands that we have faith when it's impossible for us to have faith, we have a right to challenge His justice, because that would be unjust. But it *is* possible for us to have faith because the Bible says, *"So then faith cometh by hearing, and hearing by the word of God"* (Rom. 10:17).

God tells us how faith comes or how we can increase our faith — by hearing His Word. Therefore, the responsibility rests with *us* whether or not we have strong faith.

Let's see what part the confession of our mouth plays in our faith walk.

> **ROMANS 10:8-10**
> **8** But what saith it? The word is nigh thee, even in thy MOUTH, and in thy HEART: that is, the word of faith, which we preach;
> **9** That if thou shalt CONFESS WITH THY MOUTH the Lord Jesus, and shalt BELIEVE IN THINE HEART that God hath raised him from the dead, thou shalt be saved.
> **10** For with the HEART man BELIEVETH unto righteousness; and with the MOUTH CONFESSION is made unto salvation.

Notice the expression, ". . . *with the mouth confes-*

sion is made unto salvation" (v. 10). That principle isn't true concerning only salvation. Actually, confession is made unto *whatsoever* — salvation, prosperity, healing, or whatever you need. This agrees exactly with what Jesus said about faith.

MARK 11:22
22 And Jesus answering saith unto them, Have faith in God.

The phrase, "Have faith in God" in the Greek literally says, "Have the faith *of* God." Or we could say it like this: "Have the God-kind of faith."

Mark 11:23 describes the God-kind of faith.

MARK 11:23
23 For verily I say unto you, That whosoever shall SAY unto this mountain, Be thou removed, and be thou cast into the sea; and shall not doubt in his heart, but shall BELIEVE that those things which he SAITH shall come to pass; he shall have whatsoever he SAITH.

I want you to notice two things here about the God-kind of faith. Number one, you need to realize that confession *precedes* possession. Most people want to possess the blessing first and *then* they'll confess it. But notice Jesus said, ". . . *he SHALL have whatsoever he SAITH"* (Mark 11:23).

You see, at the time you say it, you don't have it. That's because *confession precedes possession.* You must confess God's Word to bring the thing you desire into the realm of reality (Heb. 11:1).

Number two, you must believe your *words*. You must believe in your heart that what you say *will* come to pass. You must believe the Word of God in your heart and then you must believe the Word of God on your lips. Doing that gives you power over demons, diseases, and circumstances.

Many times people will say, "Oh, I wish I had that kind of faith." Well, the Bible says you do! Second Corinthians 4:13 says, *"We having the same spirit of faith. . . ."*

The Apostle Paul didn't say we are *trying* to get the same spirit of faith or we are *hoping* to get it. He didn't say someday we *might* get it. Paul said in Second Corinthians, *"having* the same spirit of faith." That's present tense. That means we have that same spirit of faith *now*.

What is this spirit of faith that we have?

2 CORINTHIANS 4:13
13 We having the same spirit of faith, according as it written, I BELIEVED, and therefore have I SPOKEN; we also BELIEVE, and therefore SPEAK.

We *believe* and *therefore we speak*. Believing and speaking the Word is operating in the same principle of faith Jesus talked about in Mark 11:23.

We can see this principle in a number of illustrations in the Word of God. The woman with the issue of blood *said, ". . . If I may but touch his garment, I shall be whole"* (Matt. 9:21). Jesus replied, *". . . Daughter, be of good comfort; THY FAITH hath made thee whole"*

(v. 22). She got exactly what she *believed* and what she *said*.

In the Old Testament, Caleb and Joshua had that same spirit of faith. *"And Caleb stilled the people before Moses, and SAID, Let us go up at once, and possess it; for WE ARE WELL ABLE to overcome it"* (Num. 13:30). The other ten men who went with Caleb and Joshua to spy out the land *said, ". . . WE BE NOT ABLE to go up against the people; for they are stronger than we"* (v. 31).

All of the spies got what they said they would get. The ten who said they weren't able to overcome, *didn't* overcome. They *said, ". . . Would God that we had died in . . . this wilderness!"* (Num. 14:2). They got what they said — they eventually died in the wilderness!

However, Caleb and Joshua *didn't* die in the wilderness. They *said, ". . . we are well able to overcome it"* (Num. 13:30). They were the only two out of that generation who entered in and possessed the Promised Land!

These are just a few of the many examples in the Word that show us that, good or bad, our words dominate our lives. So don't ever talk failure or defeat. Never for one moment admit that God can't cause you to overcome in life. When you talk defeat, you are saying, "God cannot put me over." But God is the God who is *more* than enough! He *can* put you over in every situation in life!

We as Christians need to become God-inside minded. We need to continually proclaim with our words that *". . . greater is he that is in you, than he that is in the world"* (1 John 4:4). The Holy Ghost that's in us is greater than the devil and the entire host of demons that are in the world. In Jesus we are *more* than conquerors over *all* the power of the enemy (Rom. 8:37)!

Learn this: Your words can put you over in life. Your words will make you a victor or they will keep you a captive. Remember, you are *snared* by the negative words that come out of your mouth (Prov. 6:2).

Your words can be filled with faith that will stir Heaven and bless humanity, or they can be filled with bitterness, hatred, or doubt. To say it a little differently, your words can become what you wish them to be. It's up to you; it's not up to anyone else.

Your faith will never register above the words of your mouth. You should fill your words with faith and love!

Cultivate the habit of dwelling upon the things of God in your thought life (Phil. 4:8). Learn to use words that will edify your own spirit — words that are positive and faith-filled.

Have you ever visited someone who was going through a test or a trial and all they talked about was doubt, unbelief, and failure? You probably went away feeling like a spirit of depression was trying to attach itself to you. Well, if what others say affects you, how much more will what *you* say affect you?

What should you talk about then? You should be talking about how big God is. When you talk about how big God is, your spirit will be buoyed up in faith, confidence, and assurance.

So many Christians defeat themselves by spending

long hours telling others how many mistakes they've made, how great their problems are, and how weak their faith is. The more they talk this way, the bigger their problems look and the weaker their faith becomes.

Instead of diagnosing your own case by looking at it through natural eyes, let God's Word diagnose your case. Believe and speak what God's Word says. Instead of saying, "I don't have much faith," say, "I have the same spirit of faith according as it is written, I believe therefore I speak" (2 Cor. 4:13).

When believers tell me that they don't have any faith, I always say to them, "Then why don't you get saved?" They say, "Oh, I *am* saved." I reply, "How in the world did you get saved without any faith, when the Bible says, *'For by grace are ye saved THROUGH FAITH . . .'* [Eph. 2:8]?. You can't be saved any other way!"

Actually, the Bible says that God has dealt to *every* believer the *measure* of faith.

ROMANS 12:3
3 **For I say, through the grace given unto me, to every man that is among you, not to think of himself more highly than he ought to think; but to think soberly, according as GOD HATH DEALT TO EVERY MAN THE MEASURE OF FAITH.**

Even as a teenager before I got into full-time ministry, I found that when I faced hard situations or crises, it helped me to say, "I have a measure of the mountain-moving faith."

At times, the going was tough and circumstances piled up on me. It looked like nothing was going right. At times, it looked like I was defeated and that failure was at the door! But I would just say out loud, "I've got a measure of the God-kind of faith; I've got a measure of the kind of faith that created the world in the beginning."

After I said that, those circumstances seemed so little and insignificant that I was ready to walk on top of all of them! My faith rose to the level of my confession!

Once you understand that everyone has a measure of the God-kind of faith, you need to realize that this faith can be increased. The Bible says, *"We are bound to thank God always for you, brethren, as it is meet, because that YOUR FAITH GROWETH exceedingly ..."* (2 Thess. 1:3). So we see that faith can grow. And it *should* grow.

The Word of God is faith food. You need to feed upon the Word and exercise your faith in order for your faith to grow. And a part of growing in faith is learning to fill your mouth with words that are in line with God's Word.

I remember when my wife and I bought our first house many years ago. It was just a little frame house, but at that time it was like a mansion to us.

My wife, Oretha, said to me, "Kenneth, we need new drapes." I told her, "I've stretched my faith as far as it will go. If you put drapes on top of my faith where it's at now, it will burst." My faith was stretched like a rubber band, just as far as it would go, to buy that house.

So I said, "Honey, if you want drapes, you'll have to believe for them." Well, Oretha put her faith out for the new drapes and began to confess the Word and build her faith. And she got those new drapes! I simply couldn't add that to my measure of faith, because I knew I was already operating up to my measure or my full capacity of faith.

If you're not sure where your level of faith is, don't try to start at the top; just start on the bottom rung of the ladder and climb up. If you can't believe for a dollar, start believing for a dime. After a while you'll get to the dollar mark.

George Mueller was a minister who built an orphanage in Bristol, England, many years ago. He once said that when he first started praying and believing God to meet the needs of the orphanage, it took all the faith he had to believe God for one dollar. But Mueller said that after fifty years of feeding his faith daily on the Word of God and exercising it, he could believe God just as easily for a million dollars as he had believed for one dollar fifty years earlier.

Many people make the mistake of trying to rise immediately to the million-dollar faith mark. Several years ago, the Lord said to me, "Get back to the ABC's of faith. So many who are teaching faith and confession today are teaching it at the level where *they* are living now. People who listen to these faith teachers try to make their faith work on that level, and they end up in a mess."

The Lord continued, "Those people don't realize that the faith teacher himself didn't start out at that level. He started out small and continued to increase his faith

by feeding on the Word and exercising it on things he
could believe for."

So there is a growth to faith. However, *whatever* a
person is believing for, the words he speaks *after* he has
prayed can determine whether or not he receives his
answer. Some people say, "Well, if I said I'm not doubting, I'd be lying about it." They are speaking what their
mind is telling them instead of listening to their spirit.
That's often what defeats people.

But faith is not of the head — it's of the heart. The
Bible says Mark 11:23 says, *"For verily I say unto you,
That whosoever shall say unto this mountain, Be
thou removed, and be thou cast into the sea; and
SHALL NOT DOUBT in his HEART, but SHALL
BELIEVE. . . ."* Shall not doubt where? Look at Romans
10:10. *"For with the HEART man BELIEVETH. . . ."*

I've said this for years, and I'm going to keep on saying it: Faith will work in your heart with doubt in your
head.

The problem is many people never distinguish
between their soul and their spirit. Faith is not of the
soul or of the mind. It is of the spirit or the heart. You
don't walk by what's in your head when it comes to the
things of God and the things you're believing — you
walk by your *spirit.*

I know faith will work in your heart with doubt in
your head. Right after I prayed the prayer of faith while
lying on that bed of sickness, my head was filled with
thoughts of doubt. My mind kept telling me, *Your
prayer of faith won't work. If you try to get up, you're*

going to fall down dead.

But I heard the Lord say to me on the inside, in my spirit, "Do you believe you're well?"

I said, "I sure do."

The Lord said, "Well, get up then! Well people ought to be up at 10:30 in the morning."

My mind said, *But how are you going to get up when you're paralyzed?* However, I didn't pay any attention to my head. I acted from my spirit and received what I had asked for in faith — I got up from that bed healed!

Some of the greatest financial miracles I've ever had in my life and ministry came about while my head was telling me, "It's not going to work. It's not going to work." But I didn't pay any attention to my head. I paid attention to my spirit and spoke what my heart believed according to the Word.

For example, that's how we bought our first house — the one that I had to use all my faith to receive. Someone offered to sell me a house if I could give him a thousand-dollar down payment within ten days. The man offered me a good deal, and I believed it was God's will for me to buy the house. So even though I didn't have the thousand dollars for a down payment, I said by faith, "I'll take it."

I told the man, "I'll have the down payment for you in ten days." I knew I had to say it! I didn't feel like saying it. In fact, my head was giving me fits.

I know it doesn't seem big now, but that one thousand dollars looked as big to me then as a million dol-

lars does today! My head told me, *It's not going to work.*
You're getting too far out on a limb. Where are you going
to get a thousand dollars! But I didn't listen to my head;
I listened to my spirit.

You've got to keep saying what you believe in your
spirit because you release your faith with the words of
your mouth. Your words will affect your circumstances.
Your words will dominate the circumstances of your life.

So before I left, I told that man several times that I
would give him the thousand dollars in ten days. I
knew I had to keep saying it.

My head fought me every step of the way. I didn't
know where I was going to get a thousand dollars in ten
days. Thoughts of failure fired at my mind faster than a
machine gun fires bullets. But I kept saying to myself,
I'll have the thousand dollars in ten days. I had learned
long before not to pay any attention to my head, but to
act from my heart or my spirit.

The next day after my morning service, a woman
who had been filled with the Holy Spirit in one of my
previous meetings called me at the parsonage and
asked me, "Do you need a thousand dollars?"

I answered, "Why do you ask?" I wanted to see if
anyone had told her that I needed a thousand dollars.

"Well," she said, "last night as I began to pray, something on the inside of me seemed to tell me to give you a
thousand dollars."

I said, "I don't doubt it, Sister."

Soon the woman came by the parsonage and handed

me ten one hundred dollar bills! Praise God, I *know* faith will work in your heart with doubt in your head!

So we see that faith is of the heart, and one way faith is released is by the words of your mouth.

But you'll have to build your faith with the word of God before it will produce for you. For example, you can always locate where people are in their faith walk by what they say. What are they *confessing*? Do they confess God's Word, or do they confess their problems?

For instance, many times I've ministered the Word and prayed with people for their healing. But I could tell by what some of them said that they weren't in faith; they weren't confessing the Word. I'd try to get them to come up to my level of faith and confession so they could agree with me that they were healed according to the Word of God. But many of these people persisted in confessing the problem instead of the Word and grew worse.

I remember one woman in particular who needed an operation. I could tell by this woman's words — her confession — that she wasn't able to believe that healing belonged to her and that according to God's Word, she was healed. So I asked her, "What *can* you believe for?"

Sometimes you have to ask people, "What can you believe for?" in order to locate them. You've got to realize that your faith will always work for you, but you can't always make your faith work for someone else. We should want to help people no matter what level of faith they are at.

So I asked this woman what she could believe for. If

she wasn't able to get in agreement with me and confess what the Word said, then I was going to get in
agreement with her! The woman said, "I can believe
that God will see me through the operation safely."

So I met her on her level of faith and agreed with
her in prayer. We prayed that she would come through
the operation and mend and recuperate so quickly that
even the doctors would be astounded. And God
answered her because she believed He would.

I was there when the doctor came by to follow up on
her after the operation. He didn't know Jesus as his
personal Savior, but he said to me, "Reverend, if
another doctor had told me that anyone with that kind
of operation had come out of it so quickly, I wouldn't
have believed it!

"I'll be honest with you," the doctor said, pointing to
her room, "that's nothing short of a miracle in there!"

Well, if you can't get the big miracle, get the little
one. Then keep exercising your faith and speaking the
Word out of your mouth — and eventually you'll have
the faith to believe for God's best!

A man once asked me, "Brother Hagin, how can I
tell whether I'm confessing the Word out of my heart or
just out of head?"

I asked him, "Are you married?"

"Yes," he replied.

I asked him, "Do you ever tell your wife you love
her?"

"Why, certainly," he answered, "I told her I loved her

just this morning at the breakfast table."

"Did that come out of your heart or your head?" I asked him.

"Oh, I get it!" the man said. When he told his wife he loved her, his heart agreed with the words he spoke.

You've got to believe the Word in your heart and then say what you believe. You can't speak the Word out of your head and expect results, because faith is of the heart.

Realize that your words dominate you. Whether your words are filled with faith or doubt, they will dominate the circumstances of your life. Your words will make you a victor or they will keep you a captive.

So learn to talk in line with the Word of God. Confess the scriptures over and over that promise you the things you desire. As you do, those scriptures will register on your spirit. Your faith will rise to the level of your confession, and you'll experience victory over your circumstances — because faith in God works!

Chapter 22
Walking With God

And Enoch lived sixty and five years, and begat Methuselah:

And Enoch walked with God after he begat Methuselah three hundred years, and begat sons and daughters:

And all the days of Enoch were three hundred sixty and five years:

And ENOCH WALKED WITH GOD: and he was not; for God took him.

— Genesis 5:21-24

By faith Enoch was translated that he should not see death; and was not found, because God had translated him: for before his translation he had this testimony, that HE PLEASED GOD.

But without faith it is impossible to please him. . . .

— Hebrews 11:5,6

Genesis chapter 5 gives us a genealogy of the patriarchs of old. Beginning with Adam, you can read how long each patriarch lived and how old he was when he died. But when you reach Genesis 5:21, you'll find an important difference in the account of the patriarch, Enoch. Enoch didn't die! Instead, the Bible says, ". . . *Enoch WALKED WITH GOD: and HE WAS NOT;*

for GOD TOOK HIM" (Gen. 5:24).

Genesis 6:5 describes the conditions Enoch lived in when he walked with God: *"And God saw that the wickedness of man was great in the earth, and that every imagination of the thoughts of his heart was only evil continually."*

Considering those conditions, Enoch must have shone as a star in the midst of the darkness. He must have been like an oasis of righteousness in a great desert of wickedness.

What made Enoch stand out so? It was that he *walked with God!*

What does the phrase, "Enoch walked with God" mean? First, Enoch walked in *divine direction!*

We often talk about receiving direction from God. But the first step to receiving guidance and direction is to choose to walk *with* God. In other words, we must choose to follow *God's* plans and purposes for our lives instead of our own plans and ambitions.

As you walk with God, you can have continual fellowship with Him. You can talk to Him as a loving Father and listen to your heart as He talks to you. You just need to trust Him, and He'll show you what you need to do.

Walking in divine direction means keeping in step with God. Enoch walked *with* God. He kept pace with God. He didn't lag behind, and he didn't run out ahead of God.

In my younger days when I received a revelation concerning God's plans for me in the future, sometimes I would just run off with it. Although it was actually something God wanted me to do, I'd run out ahead of Him.

I hadn't learned yet that even though God may begin to deal with me about taking a new direction in His plan for me, that doesn't mean I should immediately stop what I'm doing and start pursuing that new direction. Keeping in step with God's *timing* is as important as walking with Him in His *will*.

Then Jesus said something to me in a vision that helped correct me. He told me, "I would rather that you be too slow than that you be too fast when acting on what I show you."

Jesus really doesn't want us to be either too fast *or* too slow to obey Him. But as He explained to me, "If you are too fast, you get out ahead of me. You're not walking with me or behind me. That means you'll lose direction. At least if you are walking *behind* Me, I'm still leading you."

We should endeavor to learn how to stay right in step with God, obeying His will and moving in His timing as we walk in His divine direction for our lives.

Second, Enoch walked in *agreement with God.* Amos 3:3 says, *"Can two walk together, except they be agreed?"* The answer, of course, is *no.* So the fact that Enoch walked with God means he also walked in *agreement* with Him.

God isn't going to agree with your plans and opinions that don't line up with His Word and His will — so you might as well go ahead and agree with God. A certain pastor I knew learned that lesson.

This pastor of a certain Full Gospel church was concerned because his church wasn't growing as it should. He decided to spend some time waiting before God in prayer and fasting to find out what was wrong.

The pastor told me that after several days of seeking God, the Lord spoke to him. The Lord said, "I'll tell you where you're missing it. You always make all your own plans for the church, then you come to Me and ask Me to bless them. Why don't you come to Me *first* and find out what I want you to do? Find out what *My* plan is and then follow it, and you'll see your church grow."

So the pastor began to walk in agreement with *God's* plan for the church, instead of pursuing his own ideas. And in a few months, instead of a congregation of about one hundred people, the church was running about five hundred in attendance.

Most of us at one time or another have made the mistake this pastor did. We've made our plans and then asked God to bless them. But if we're going to walk with God, we must make the decision to continually seek Him and to get in agreement with *His* will for our lives.

Third, Enoch walked with God *in faith.* Hebrews 11:5 says, *"BY FAITH Enoch was translated . . . for before his translation he had this testimony, that HE PLEASED GOD."*

We all know we can trust God. But the outstanding characteristic about Enoch was that God could trust *him!* Enoch pleased God with his *faith.*

There's no doubt about the fact that we can trust God. But can God trust us? Is He pleased with us? The first phrase of Hebrews 11:5 is: *"By faith. . . ."* The last phrase is: *". . . he* [Enoch] *pleased God."* Those two phrases put together tell the story of Enoch: "By faith Enoch pleased God."

Then notice the next verse: *"But WITHOUT FAITH IT IS IMPOSSIBLE TO PLEASE HIM: for he that cometh to God must believe that he is, and that he is a rewarder of them that diligently seek him."* There is something about faith which pleases God. If we want to walk with God, the only way we can do it is *by faith.*

There's something else about Enoch that I want to point out. Enoch lived his life day by day, walking with God — until one day, he just walked right into Heaven with Him.

The Bible teaches that in the last days, something similar will occur when believers are caught away to Heaven in what is commonly called the Rapture or the catching away of the Church to Heaven (1 Cor. 15:51-54; 1 Thess. 4:16,17). Many believe that Enoch is a type of the Rapture of the Church. I'm of that opinion myself.

In Genesis 5, we read that Enoch was taken away to Heaven. Then in Genesis 6, we read the account of God's judgment on the wickedness of the world. God destroyed the earth by water. But before He did, Enoch was taken out.

Another Day of Judgment is coming. This time the

earth will be destroyed by fire. But just as Enoch was taken out before the Great Flood, so the Church will be caught away to Heaven or "raptured" before that great Day of Judgment.

When we talk about the Rapture, some folks say, "That word 'rapture' isn't even in the Bible." That's true. But the Bible does talk about the event which we commonly call the Rapture — the catching away of the Church.

> **1 THESSALONIANS 4:16,17**
> **16 For the Lord himself shall descend from heaven with a shout, with the voice of the archangel, and with the trump of God: and the dead in Christ shall rise first:**
> **17 Then we which are alive and remain shall be CAUGHT UP together with them in the clouds to meet the Lord in the air: and so shall we ever be with the Lord.**

One of the dictionary definitions of the word, "rapture," is *the carrying or transporting of a person to another place or sphere of existence.* That's what First Thessalonians 4:16,17 is talking about. There will come a day when the Church is going to be supernaturally transported to another sphere of existence — the Heaven of heavens!

We know in that sense Enoch was raptured. He was caught away. He was transported from one place to another — from the earth to Heaven.

I believe there is coming a "catching away" of the saints of God. and I believe even now we are in the last days. As never before, *we need to walk with God.*

Enoch lived in a different day than we do; and he walked under a different covenant. Here are some important things the New Testament teaches about walking with God.

First, just as Enoch did, we are to *walk by faith.* The New Testament says we are to ". . . *walk in the steps of that faith of our father Abraham . . ."* (Rom. 4:12).

Our walk with God under the New Covenant begins with the first "step of faith" — the new birth: *"For by grace are ye SAVED THROUGH FAITH . . ."* (Eph. 2:8). After we have taken the first step of faith and have been born again, Second Corinthians 5:7 says we are to *walk* by faith and not by sight.

To "walk by sight" means to live according to our physical senses and mental reasonings. We face a constant battle between our flesh and our spirit in this life as we endeavor to walk by faith instead of by sight.

Romans 4:12 says we are to walk in the steps of Abraham, who is the father of our faith. How did Abraham walk by faith?

God promised to give Abraham a son, even though Abraham was one hundred and Sarah was ninety years old. And Abraham believed the promise of God, even when all natural circumstances looked contrary to God's word to him.

Common sense told Abraham no one as old as he and Sarah could become parents. But God had given Abraham a promise, and Abraham ". . . *staggered not at*

*the promise of God through unbelief; but was strong in
faith, giving glory to God"* (Rom. 4:20).

Certainly there are some times in life when we must
walk by common sense. For instance, we better have
enough common sense not to step out in front of an
oncoming car!

However, in spiritual matters, common sense often
contradicts what God has said in His Word. And Christians often have become so accustomed to walking by
common sense that they don't walk by faith. Therefore,
they fail to receive God's blessings.

When God has spoken — and He has spoken to us
in His Word — we are to walk in faith, even if what He
has said contradicts common sense.

Second, the New Testament walk with God is a
walk in the spirit.

ROMANS 8:1
**1 There is therefore now no condemnation to
them which are in Christ Jesus, who walk not
after the flesh, but after the Spirit.**

In the original Greek of the New Testament, there is
only one word for spirit — the Greek word "pneuma."
The translators had to decide from the passage whether
it referred to the Holy Spirit or the human spirit.

I'm fully convinced that the translators of the *King
James Version* sometimes erroneously capitalized the
letter "s" in the word "spirit," making it refer to the
Holy Spirit when it actually refers to the *human* spirit.

I believe Romans 8:1 is an example of this. I believe this scripture actually means that rather than letting your *flesh* dominate you, you should let your *spirit man* dominate.

You see, it is the inward man that has become a new creature (2 Cor. 5:17). It is within our *spirit* that the Holy Spirit comes to dwell (1 Cor. 3:16). So to walk with God means to walk according to our *spirit* and not according to dictates of the flesh.

Walk according to your spirit nature. Let your inward man dominate you, not the outward man or the flesh.

Third, as New Testament believers we are to *walk in the light*.

> **1 JOHN 1:7**
> **7 But if we WALK IN THE LIGHT, as he is in the light, we have fellowship one with another, and the blood of Jesus Christ his Son cleanseth us from all sin.**

What does it mean to "walk in the light"?

The Bible says, *"The entrance of THY WORDS giveth LIGHT . . ."* (Ps. 119:130). Another scripture says, *"Thy WORD is a LAMP unto my feet, and a LIGHT unto my path"* (Ps. 119:105). The entrance of God's Word enlightens us. When the Bible talks about walking in the light, it means for us to *walk in the light of God's Word*.

You simply can't walk with God under the New Covenant without walking according to the Word. Enoch walked with God under a different covenant. He didn't have the written Word like we do, yet he walked with God. How much more should we be able to walk with God when He has given us His Holy written Word! We are to feed upon the Word of God daily and walk in the light of its truth.

Fourth, as New Testament believers we are *to walk in fellowship with God and with one another.*

When we walk in the light, the blood of Jesus cleanses us from all sin so we can walk in fellowship with God the Father and with His Son, Jesus Christ (1 John 1:3,7). We can continually fellowship with Them through the Word and through prayer.

Sin will block your fellowship with God. When you allow sin in your life, you are not walking in the light of the Word. But First John 1:9 says, *"If we CONFESS our sins, he is faithful and just to FORGIVE us our sins, and to CLEANSE us from all unrighteousness."*

If you know you have sinned, immediately confess your sin to God and get back in fellowship with Him. As long as you stay in fellowship with Him and walk in the light, the blood of Jesus perpetually and continually cleanses you of sin!

And when we walk in the light of the Word and in fellowship with the Father and Jesus, we are also in fellowship with one another. That's what First John 1:7 says: *". . . if we walk in the light, as he is in the light, WE HAVE FELLOWSHIP ONE WITH ANOTHER. . . ."*

This is a hard saying, but true: *The man or woman who is not in fellowship with fellow Christians is not walking in the light and is not walking with God.* If we walk in the light as He is in the light we have fellowship, not only with Him, but with one another.

I make it my business to maintain the right kind of fellowship and relationship toward God's people because we're all a part of the same Body.

We might not agree on every point of doctrine. But if we exalt Jesus Christ as the Son of God, we are a part of the same spiritual family, and we need each other.

Sometimes believers get into error by isolating themselves from the rest of the Body of Christ for one reason or another. People who do that are *not* walking with God!

But Hebrews 10:25 says, *"Not forsaking the assembling of ourselves together, as the manner of some is; but exhorting one another: and so much the more, as ye see THE DAY approaching."* The "day that is approaching" refers to the day of the Second Coming of Jesus Christ on this earth. As we see that day approaching, we need to assemble ourselves together and exhort one another even more!

We need one another. And we need to walk in love one toward another — not only those of our own particular fellowship — but toward *all* fellow Christians.

When I get to the end of my life, I'd like people to be able to say about me what they said about Enoch: "He walked with God." Could people say that about you?

The time is short. That day is fast approaching when Jesus will return to this earth. Today more than ever, we need to learn how to *walk with God!*

Chapter 23
The Glory of God

It came even to pass, as the trumpeters and singers were as one, to make one sound to be heard in praising and thanking the Lord; and when they lifted up their voice with the trumpets and cymbals and instruments of musick, and praised the Lord, saying, For he is good; for his mercy endureth for ever: that then the house was filled with a cloud, even the house of the Lord;

So that THE PRIESTS COULD NOT STAND to minister by reason of the cloud: FOR THE GLORY OF THE LORD HAD FILLED THE HOUSE OF GOD.

— 2 Chronicles 5:13,14

Have you ever been among a gathering of believers where the Presence of the Holy Spirit was so strong people were not even able to stand? I have, many times. I don't know about you, but I am hungry to see more of the glory of God manifested in our midst. That's what God wants. He is growing us up spiritually as a Body so we will usher in His manifested Presence more and more when we come together to worship and magnify His Name.

What are we talking about when we refer to "the glory of God"? Let's compare two scriptures to find an answer to that question. The Bible states that it was the *glory of the Father* which raised Jesus from the dead: *". . . CHRIST WAS RAISED UP from the dead BY THE GLORY OF THE FATHER . . ."* (Rom. 6:4). But the Bible also says the *Holy Spirit* raised Jesus from the dead: *". . . the SPIRIT OF HIM that RAISED UP JESUS from the dead . . ."* (Rom. 8:11). So the glory of the Lord *is* the manifestation of the Holy Spirit.

Throughout the Old and New Testaments, the Bible gives different instances of God revealing His glory to man by the power of the Holy Spirit. Let's look at a few biblical accounts where God manifested His glory to His people.

> EXODUS 40:34,35
> 34 Then a CLOUD covered the tent of the congregation, and THE GLORY OF THE LORD FILLED THE TABERNACLE.
> 35 And Moses was not able to enter into the tent of the congregation, because the CLOUD abode thereon, and THE GLORY OF THE LORD filled the tabernacle.

> ISAIAH 6:1,4
> 1 In the year that king Uzziah died I saw also the Lord sitting upon a throne, high and lifted up, and his train filled the temple. . . .
> 4 And THE POSTS OF THE DOOR MOVED at the voice of him that cried, and THE HOUSE WAS FILLED WITH SMOKE.

> EZEKIEL 1:28
> 28 As the appearance of the bow that is in the cloud in the day of rain, so was the appearance of the BRIGHTNESS round about. This was the appearance of the likeness of the GLORY OF THE

LORD. And when I [Ezekiel] saw it, I fell upon my face, and I heard a voice of one that spake.

EZEKIEL 10:4
4 Then the GLORY OF THE LORD went up from the cherub, and stood over the threshold of the house; and the house was filled with the CLOUD, and the court was full of the BRIGHTNESS of the LORD'S GLORY.

LUKE 9:28,29,32,34
28 And it came to pass about an eight days after these sayings, he [Jesus] took Peter and John and James, and went up into a mountain to pray.
29 And as he prayed, the fashion of his countenance was altered, and his raiment was WHITE and GLISTERING [glistening]. . . .
32 But Peter and they that were with him were heavy with sleep: and when they were awake, THEY SAW HIS GLORY, and the two men [Moses and Elijah] that stood with him. . . .
34 . . . there came a CLOUD, and overshadowed them: and they feared as they entered into the CLOUD.

I want you to notice that several words are used to describe the manifestation of God's glory. For instance, again and again we read the words "cloud" and "smoke" in the same context as "the glory of God" (Exod. 16:10; 24:16; 40:34,35; Num. 16:42; 1 Kings 8:11; Isa. 4:5). Also, the words *brightness, white,* and *glistering* are used to describe certain manifestations of God's glory (Ezek. 1:28; 10:4; Luke 9:29). In other scriptures, the words *shine* and *light* are used in connection with God's manifested glory (Matt. 17:2; Acts 22:6,11).

Throughout my ministry, I have experienced the Presence of the Holy Spirit manifested in ways similar to the scriptures we just read. For instance, many times I have seen the glory of God manifested in the form of a cloud. Sometimes I will look over the crowd as I'm preaching and I'll see the glory cloud just as a haze of smoke hanging right over their heads. Other times it is manifested in a greater measure, even to such an extent that I can't see a thing while I am inside the cloud of God's glory.

For instance, once as a young Baptist boy preacher I was preaching on the street, and I experienced a powerful manifestation of the glory cloud. This was during Depression Days when there weren't many jobs and a lot of people would congregate on the streets with nothing else to do. I announced that I was going to preach, and in a short time I had myself quite a crowd, eager to hear what I had to say. I began to preach hard and fast and got through about two thirds of my sermon, when the glory cloud came down on me.

When that cloud comes into a building, it usually fills the entire building. But because I was out in the open preaching, it just came down and enveloped me. I couldn't see anyone; I couldn't even see the microphone I was holding! I could hear the sound of my voice, but I couldn't distinguish the words I was speaking. I was caught up in the realm of the Spirit.

After about thirty minutes, the glory cloud began lifting and I could see the people I was preaching to. However, I didn't know what I had preached about for the past thirty minutes, so I just said, "Let's bow our heads and pray."

I gave the invitation for anyone who wanted to get saved to come forward, and twelve grown men responded. That may not seem like many people in this day, but in those days it was a landslide!

Sometimes in my meetings the glory cloud will come as I am about to minister to people in a healing line. The first time that happened I was holding a meeting for Brother Gordon Lindsay in the 1960's.

I had laid hands on about half of the people in the healing line. Then I saw the glory cloud rolling into the building. I walked back to the pulpit because I knew in that instance if I stood in that cloud, I would fall under the power of the Holy Spirit along with the rest of the people.

The cloud came floating over the heads of the congregation. Meanwhile, the people in the healing line all had their eyes closed and were worshipping God. They weren't watching me.

I waited until the cloud was right above the people in the healing line, and then I waved my hand. When I did that, every person in the healing line fell down like dominoes under the power of the Spirit. The people in the healing line were experiencing the power of the Holy Spirit, just as the priests did when God's glory filled the temple and they could not stand up to minister (2 Chron. 5:13,14),

Let's look at another way the glory of God can be manifested. In Acts 9, the account of Saul's encounter with Jesus on the road to Damascus shows us that the glory of God can be manifested as *light*.

As Saul traveled to Damascus on a mission to persecute Christians, he was arrested in his journey by a light from Heaven that shone round about him (Acts 9:3). Later Paul relates that experience to a crowd in Jerusalem, saying, "... *I could not see for the GLORY of that LIGHT* ..." (Acts 22:11). You see, Saul wasn't blinded by a physical impairment in his eyes. He was blinded for a time because the glory of God came upon him.

I have had several experiences in which the glory of God was manifested as a blinding light. For instance, in 1940, the congregation I was pastoring in north central Texas experienced that manifestation of God's glory. A young minister who was a converted Jew had been holding revival meetings in my church for about three weeks.

The young Jewish man was about to give the altar call when suddenly a blinding light flashed across the sanctuary. For a moment no one could see anything. Just as quickly as it came, the light was gone, and there were people down at the altar getting saved!

Many people in the congregation later told me, "We don't know how those people got down to the altar! They would have had to walk past us to get to the aisle, but we know they didn't go by us."

So how did those people get down to the altar in that split second as that light from Heaven flashed? No one knows to this day, except God. You talk about "signs and wonders"! That was a sign and a wonder, wasn't it!

God desires to demonstrate His glory and power upon this earth today, just as He did in the Bible. I am of the opinion that God wants to manifest His power and glory more today than He has been able to, and He is endeavoring to get the Body of Christ to a position where He can do that.

In this generation, we've received revelation from the Word about the baptism of the Holy Spirit and speaking in other tongues. But it seems to me that we've stopped at the door to the supernatural realm of God. There is so much more to experience in the realm of God's Spirit.

I'm not talking about fanaticism. But I'm saying we have only gotten to the edge of that realm of the Spirit where God's glory dwells. It's like dipping our toes in the water a little and then jumping around shouting, "Isn't this wonderful!"

But God wants us to go a little deeper into the water. In other words, He wants us to learn to operate supernaturally in the realm of the Spirit. As we learn how to do that, God will have more freedom to demonstrate His glory and power in a greater measure upon this earth.

One key to experiencing more manifestations of God's glory can be found in the account of the dedication of Solomon's temple. In that instance, as *God's people worshipped in one accord*, the manifestation of God's glory was ushered in: "*. . . as the trumpeters and singers were AS ONE, to make one sound to be heard in*

*praising and thanking the Lord . . . that THEN the
house was FILLED WITH A CLOUD, even the house of
the Lord"* (2 Chron. 5:13).

As the people became *as one* in praising and worshipping the Lord, *then* God's glory filled the house of
God. The same principle applies today under the New
Covenant. Under the New Covenant, God dwells in His
people, not in a literal, physical building (2 Cor. 6:16).
And as believers cooperate with the Spirit of God and
get into one accord when they come together to worship,
they open the way for God to manifest His glory.

Many times we emphasize that the Holy Spirit
indwells the individual believer and helps him in life.
And that is scriptural, for the Bible calls each believer
the temple of the living God (1 Cor. 3:16). Every
believer has an *individual* anointing — the Person of
the Holy Spirit — abiding within (1 John 2:20,27).

But there is also a *corporate* anointing, which is
much stronger than the individual anointing. And the
corporate anointing will come into greatest manifestation when believers get in one accord.

In Solomon's day, there was a physical building
called the house of God. Under the New Covenant, we
as believers are called the house of God (Heb. 3:6).
When we come together as a body of believers, we form
a spiritual house. And if we will just get into unity, we
can bring the glory and power of God on the scene (Acts
2:1-4; 4:24-31; 5:12).

From 1937 to 1949, I pastored several churches. But
I was only able to get one congregation — the church in

Farmersville, Texas — to that place of unity in worship which brings the glory of God into manifestation because of the corporate anointing. I was never able to get another congregation I pastored to that place of worship.

However, one time in the last church I pastored in Van, Texas, I was able to get the people to the place where the glory of God was manifested in our midst. Our church and another church were holding a fellowship meeting together, and I was preaching. The building was full, and the people were with me in such unity in the Spirit that God could powerfully manifest His glory.

I had just finished my message. I gave an utterance in tongues by the unction of the Holy Spirit, and the other pastor on the platform got up and gave the interpretation. The interpretation was about believers being in one accord.

Suddenly, it was as if a strong wind blew through the building. Whoosh! Everyone in the church heard it! We experienced a manifestation of the Holy Ghost similar to what the believers in the Upper Room experienced in Acts 2:2: *"And suddenly there came a sound from heaven as of A RUSHING MIGHTY WIND, and it filled all the house where they were sitting."*

When that Holy Ghost wind blew through our gathering, every sinner in the building was saved. Every backslider was restored to fellowship. Every person who had never been filled with the Holy Spirit began speaking in tongues. Every sick person was healed. The glory of God was manifested in our midst in a mighty way!

One woman had been brought to the meeting in an

ambulance and was lying against the wall on a
stretcher. She had been operated on six times. The doctors had told her she had only two months to live. This
woman's body had wasted away until she looked the
very picture of death.

No one prayed for this woman; no one touched her.
But when the Spirit of God blew through the building
like a wind, she leaped off that stretcher and ran up
and down the aisles completely healed!

When that wind blew through the building, another
woman who was just visiting the church was saved,
filled with the Holy Spirit, healed, and was delivered
from cigarettes. She had been a church member of
another denomination and had never been to a Full
Gospel service until that day.

She testified later, "Before I came to that meeting, I
thought I was saved because I had joined a church as a
child. However, I knew I was bound by the cigarette
habit and by sickness in my body. But when that wind
blew on me, I suddenly realized I had never been saved. I
gave my heart to the Lord, and I was immediately filled
with the Holy Spirit and began speaking in tongues."

The woman continued, "When I got home after the
meeting, I realized all my physical ailments had disap-
peared. And not only that, but I have never touched
another cigarette since then. The thought has never
even occurred to me to smoke again!"

Can you see what I mean about the power of the
corporate anointing? It stands to reason that when

believers come together in unity, the corporate anointing is much greater than the individual anointing that resides within each believer. That's why it is so important for believers to be in unity and in one accord when they gather together.

In these days in which we live, there are going to be more manifestations of God's glory like these I've shared. God wants to powerfully manifest His glory in our midst. I believe that more and more the Body of Christ is getting in position for Him to do that. We are almost there. In fact, I believe we are only a half a step away from it!

Let's all seek the Lord diligently and learn the ways of the Holy Spirit. Let's strive to be of one mind and one accord as a body of believers. It's time to prepare ourselves for a greater measure of the manifestation of God's power and glory to be ushered in upon this earth, so those in the world might believe in and accept our glorious risen Savior!

Chapter 24
Man and Miracles

(Keynote message of Campmeeting '78, preached from a revelation of the Holy Spirit to Kenneth E. Hagin.)

In the days before Campmeeting '78, this thought kept rolling over and over in my spirit: *Man and miracles. Man and miracles.* I want to share with you some of what I received from the Lord as I pondered those words.

Man is a spirit being who has a soul and lives in a body. He was created by a supernatural God and designed to live in God's supernatural realm on this earth.

The supernatural realm *is* the realm of the believer. The new birth itself is supernatural. Second Corinthians 5:17 says, *"Therefore if any man be in Christ, HE IS A NEW CREATURE: old things are passed away; behold, all things are become new."*

When you are born again, you still have the same body you had before. But the spirit man became a new creation — a supernatural being!

The baptism in the Holy Spirit also is supernatural. After you are born of the Spirit of God and have become a new creature in Christ, you can be filled with the Holy Spirit.

This is a supernatural experience, and it is accompanied with a supernatural sign: *"And they were all filled with the Holy Ghost, and BEGAN TO SPEAK WITH OTHER TONGUES, as the SPIRIT GAVE THEM UTTERANCE"* (Acts 2:4). Then Mark 16:17 says, *"And these SIGNS shall follow them that BELIEVE . . . they shall SPEAK with new TONGUES."* The Bible calls speaking in tongues a supernatural *sign.*

We can continue living a supernatural life in Christ by maintaining a supernatural prayer life.

As spirit beings who have been made new creatures in Christ, we have the capability to know God and commune intelligently with Him. We can have a conversation with God just as we can have a conversation with our fellow man, because God is a Person — a divine Personality and our Heavenly Father.

I left the last church I pastored in 1949 and went out into field ministry. About three years later I overheard the man who was my crusade director at that time, saying to someone else, "That fellow Hagin prays funnier than anyone I've ever heard in my life."

The man went on to say, "He and I shared an apartment during the last meeting. We each had our own bedroom. I heard him talking to someone in his room. I thought to myself, *No one went in there because I would have seen someone come down the hall. So who is Brother Hagin holding a conversation with?*

"I listened. After forty-five minutes I thought, *There must be somebody in there.* So I cracked the door and peeked in. Brother Hagin sat in the middle of the floor with his eyes shut. He would talk. Then he would listen. He'd answer back. Then he'd listen again. He would say 'Yes, that's right. That's right. Yes, I understand that.' I guess he was praying."

That's exactly what I was doing. Thank God, our spiritual nature has the capacity to know God and to commune intelligently with Him! The fellowship and communion with God that Adam lost in the Fall has been restored to us through Jesus Christ. Now it's up to us to develop our spirits so we can enjoy more intimate fellowship with the Father God and operate in His supernatural realm.

One way we develop our spirits is by praying much in other tongues. Over fifty years ago when I was baptized with the Holy Ghost and spoke with other tongues, a certain Pentecostal teaching of that day left the impression that the baptism of the Holy Spirit is the beginning and the end of the Pentecostal experience and that there is nothing more to experience. But, actually, being filled with the Holy Spirit with the evidence of speaking in other tongues is just the *door into* the supernatural.

Spirit-filled believers are supposed to live their lives communing with God on a supernatural level. The Bible says, *"For he that speaketh in an unknown tongue speaketh not unto men, but unto God: for no man understandeth him; howbeit in the spirit he speaketh mysteries"* (1 Cor. 14:2).

Notice when you pray in tongues, you are not talking to men. You are not communicating naturally;

you're communicating *supernaturally* with God. *Moffatt's* translation says when you pray in other tongues, you are ". . . talking of *divine secrets* in the Spirit."

Praying in the Spirit will develop your spirit and help bring the supernatural power of God into manifestation.

A Baptist pastor in recent times said to me, "I see in the Word that it's scriptural to pray for the sick. I conduct public healing meetings, and I lay hands on the sick in my church on Sunday nights. But I take issue with anyone who would tell me I don't have the Holy Spirit. I know I have the Holy Spirit because I'm born of the Spirit."

I said, "You're right. You're born of the Spirit, and you do have the Holy Ghost."

"Oh," he said, "I thought you were saying I didn't have the Holy Spirit because I haven't spoken in tongues."

"No," I said, "you *are* born of the Spirit of God. But have you been *filled* with the Holy Spirit?"

"I think so," the pastor answered. "How can I tell for sure if I've been filled?"

"Well," I said, "the only way I know is the Bible evidence for the infilling of the Holy Spirit that's given in Mark 16:17: '. . . these *SIGNS shall follow them that believe;* . . . *they shall speak with new tongues.'*

"Then in Acts 2:4, the Bible says, '*And they were all FILLED WITH THE HOLY GHOST, and began to SPEAK WITH OTHER TONGUES, as the Spirit gave them utterance.'* When those believers were filled with the Holy Ghost, they started talking in other tongues. That's the *Bible* evidence for being filled with the Holy Spirit."

"I want to be filled with the Holy Ghost, all right," he said, "but I don't know whether or not I want that tongues business. Has it done anything for you?"

"It sure has!" I exclaimed. "Let me tell you about it."

I explained, "As a young Baptist boy preacher, I saw God's power manifested once in a while because I learned early how to pray in faith according to Mark 11:23,24. As a teenager I prayed the prayer of faith for myself and was raised from a deathbed.

"Then I began teaching what I knew about faith to others. I laid hands on people and anointed them with oil because the Bible said to do that [James 5:14,15]. I did the best I could with what I knew, and I saw a few healed."

I continued, "But being filled with the Holy Ghost and praying in other tongues has made all the difference in the world in my own life and ministry."

Then I gave him this example. "While I was still pastoring, I was invited to preach at a fellowship meeting of my Full Gospel denomination. I got up early that day and walked up and down the aisles of the church, praying in other tongues. I was preparing myself by tuning up my spirit and getting over into the supernatural realm.

"At the fellowship meeting, I preached for about

forty minutes. Then I gave an utterance in tongues and the pastor of the host church interpreted it. All of a sudden, the power of God swept through the church like a strong wind. We could even hear it blowing through the sanctuary.

"As the power of God swept into that building, within a moment of time, every lost person in the meeting got saved. Everyone who didn't have the baptism of the Holy Spirit began speaking in tongues. Every sick person was healed. No one touched them or said anything to them!

"One woman had been rolled into the meeting on a stretcher. She'd had six operations, but doctors had told her there was nothing more they could do for her. She was dying and very near death. But when that powerful wind of the Holy Spirit blew through the church, she jumped off that stretcher and started running up and down the aisles." Glory to God! That was the supernatural power of God in demonstration!

Man has a deep-seated desire for the miraculous demonstration of God's power and glory. That's because man was created in the image of a supernatural, miracle-working God. And God has provided an entrance into the supernatural through the baptism of the Holy Spirit and by His Word.

Actually, the supernatural realm is the realm we were created to live in. Man was brought into being by a miracle-working God. And we will always yearn to see the miracle-working power of God in demonstration.

Sin has blinded us and kept us imprisoned in the

natural realm. But, thank God, the hunger for the supernatural is within our hearts. If we will seek after God, we can learn to live in the supernatural realm by the power of the Holy Spirit and the Word of God.

Many churches have backed off from the supernatural workings of God — even churches that used to believe and operate regularly in the supernatural. Now the supernatural has waned in many churches, and the miraculous is no longer in manifestation.

When churches keep the Holy Spirit from having His way in their services, they will eventually become cold and dead spiritually. When any body of believers denies the supernatural in Christianity, they begin following a dead religion of ethics, instead of experiencing a supernatural relationship with a miracle-working God.

On the other hand, there are believers who are contending for an increased manifestation of the miraculous power of God!

A leader of one of the major Full Gospel denominations said to me, "Our denomination was born in the fire of the Spirit and in the outpouring of God's supernatural power. But then in later years, manifestations of the supernatural dwindled down to almost nothing.

"Finally, as few as fifty or a hundred people attended our monthly state-wide meetings. So we held a meeting to discuss whether or not we should dispense with certain meetings because of lack of attendance."

This Full Gospel leader continued, "At the meeting, I just held my peace. Finally one minister said, 'I believe we ought to ask Brother S_____ [and he mentioned my name] what he thinks. After all, he's an elder in our midst, and he was one of the founding fathers of the Pentecostal Movement.'

"So since they asked me to comment, I did. I got up and said, 'Gentlemen, I believe we are out of order by even discussing the cancellation of meetings. I believe there is only one issue we need to talk about, and that's how we can make our meetings more spiritual. How can we bring back the manifestation of God's supernatural power into our midst?'"

This man continued, "So as a denomination, we began to seek God for the supernatural power of God to be manifested in our midst. And as God began to confirm the Word with signs following, attendance at our meetings began to increase dramatically. People whose hearts were hungry for more of God were drawn to these meetings where God's power was being demonstrated."

It was the same way in Jesus' day. People were drawn to Him because He was a miracle worker. And as ministers today preach the anointed Word and allow Jesus to work miracles in their midst, people will be drawn to come and witness the supernatural power of God!

As a young preacher, I heard Raymond T. Richey preach when I attended the Texas District Council Meetings of the Assemblies of God. I heard him say again and again: "Divine healing is the dinner bell. Keep ringing that bell and people will come."

I went back to my little church, which had a congregation of less than a hundred, and did just what Richey said. I started ringing a dinner bell every Saturday night by preaching what the Word of God said about the power of the gospel to save, deliver, and heal.

For six months nothing happened. But then we hit a gusher! The insane began to be delivered! The paralyzed were healed! People were raised up from deathbeds! And people from several neighboring counties came and filled the building every Saturday night. Glory to God!

I just kept ringing the dinner bell, and God was faithful to manifest His supernatural, delivering power. I've been ringing that bell for more than fifty years, and I'm not going to quit now. I'm going to keep on ringing it, because the Word of God works!

Jesus is as much a miracle worker today as He ever was. He has not changed. And man needs the miraculous power of God today just as much as he ever did.

Some people say, "We don't need miracles anymore." But we do! Thank God, we can act upon God's Word, and God will manifest His power just as He did in the days when Jesus walked the earth.

Jesus Christ is the same yesterday, today, and forever (Heb. 13:8). He has not changed. He is the same Jesus now as He was then. If He healed people when He walked upon this earth, He heals today. If He worked miracles then, He works miracles today.

Jesus is a miracle worker! We need to find out how He works — how to scripturally put a demand on His miracle-working power. Then we can work *with* Him and see His miraculous power manifested in our lives.

What causes Jesus to demonstrate His power with signs and miracles? We find the answer in Mark 16:20: *"And they went forth, and preached every where, the Lord working with them, and CONFIRMING THE WORD WITH SIGNS FOLLOWING. . . ."* How did the Lord work? He worked with the disciples to *confirm the Word* they preached with *signs following.*

Jesus works with us just as He worked with the Early Church. If we want to increase the manifestation of God's miraculous power in our midst, we must do what those in the Early Church did — preach the Word!

God will confirm His Word! He won't confirm a particular *preacher.* He won't confirm a *personality.* He will confirm the *Word* with signs following!

I was reading this passage in Mark 16 one day when I was pastoring my last church, and I got stirred up about it. I began to fast and pray and wait on God.

"Lord," I said, "things are comfortable in our church. The church is growing. It's financially sound. A few people are getting saved and baptized in the Holy Ghost, and a few are being healed. But as I read Mark 16, it seems to me we ought to be experiencing more supernatural signs and demonstrations of Your power than we are."

On the third day of my fast, the Lord spoke to my spirit, "I said I would confirm My Word with signs following."

I said, "I know that. That's what I'm praying and fasting about. I want to see You do it."

The Lord said again, "I said I would confirm My Word with signs following."

I said, "I know that You said You would confirm Your Word with signs following. That's what I'm trying to get You to do." (I didn't know as much back then as I do now!)

He said the third time, "I said I would confirm My *Word* with signs following."

I said, "I know that, Lord. It's written right here in Mark 16. I just read it. You said You would confirm Your Word with signs following. That's what I want You to do."

The Lord said, "Do you think I am a liar?"

I said, "Oh, no. You're not a liar."

"Well," He said, "you don't have to pray that I will do it. You don't even have to fast to get Me to do it. If you will put the Word out, I *will* confirm My Word."

Put the Word out! That's what I thought I was doing! I said, "Lord, I'm a stickler for the Word. You know me. I'm a *Word* man!"

He said, "Check up on what you're preaching."

So I checked up on what I was preaching, and I was amazed! I found out I was preaching sixty percent Word, five percent tradition, and thirty-five percent unbelief! I whacked off the unbelief instantly. But it was not as easy to get rid of the religious tradition I'd been preaching.

One day I was praying in my church and laying everything inside me on the altar — all my motives, opinions, beliefs, and ambitions — so the Lord could examine them. For example, *Why did I want to do such-and-such?*

I knew I had to get rid of all my religious traditions if I wanted the supernatural power of the Holy Spirit and the Word to work fully in my life and ministry.

Then I stopped preaching tradition and unbelief and began to teach more of the Word. Immediately we began to see results. Signs followed the Word, and the miraculous power of God began to be manifested in our church.

The early Christians didn't heal the sick and cast out devils without putting out any Word. *First* they preached the Word. *Then* the Lord worked with them to confirm the Word they preached with signs following. Find out how God works and work with Him. Then He will work with you supernaturally.

God is the Father of spirits (Heb. 12:9), and we are His children, created in His image and likeness (Gen. 1:26; 5:1).

If you are a Spirit-filled believer, the supernatural realm of God is *your* realm. You were created by a supernatural God. Your spirit was made a new creation supernaturally in the new birth. You were supernaturally filled with the Holy Spirit and were given supernatural utterance in other tongues by that same Holy Ghost.

Now it's up to you whether or not you live your life supernaturally in the power of the Holy Spirit. If you will determine to educate your spirit by diligently studying the Word of God and praying in the Holy Ghost, the supernatural realm of God will become as natural to you as water is to a fish.

It will be natural for you to operate in the supernatural realm — in the realm of the miraculous — because that is your natural realm.

In February 1943, I prayed in other tongues in my study for five hours and forty-five minutes. Then I received a word of wisdom by the Spirit. I grabbed my pencil and began to write.

Here's what the Lord said: "At the end of World War II there will come a revival of divine healing to America." We saw that divine-healing revival come. It began in 1947 and lasted until about 1958.

Then in 1958 I was holding a revival meeting in a church in Dallas, Texas. I said from the pulpit under the inspiration of the Holy Spirit: "The healing revival is waning and is about over. The next revival will be in the church."

The people thought I meant the next revival would be in the Full Gospel church. "No," I said, "the next revival will be in the *denominational* church."

As I stood on that platform, in the Spirit I saw myself preaching in Baptist churches, Methodist churches, Catholic churches, and many other denominational churches. Everything I saw has come to pass. The Charismatic Movement swept through denominational churches during the '60s and '70s. During those two decades, I preached in all those churches I had seen in the Spirit that day in 1958.

Then in July 1978, I saw in the Spirit what the next move of God would be. We're still in the middle of that move.

I saw there was going to be a return of the supernatural on the earth. And I saw that the prophet's ministry in the days ahead would come more into manifestation.

The prophet is a seer. He sees into the realm of the Spirit. He stands very often on the horizon of time and sees into two worlds — the spirit world and the natural world. He interprets into the natural world what he sees in the spirit world. That's where I stood in 1943, 1958, and 1978, when I prophesied about the coming moves of God.

I heard myself say, "In the coming revival, there's going to be *increased manifestations of the supernatural.* These manifestations won't be something new, although it will be new to many folks who have never operated in God's supernatural realm. These supernatural manifestations will always be in line with the Word of God.

"In this move of God, people who are called to the office of the prophet will stand in that office and minister in many ways they should have been ministering before. The glory of God will come down upon whole congregations until the whole building will be filled with a glory cloud that many will be able to see. There will be people who fall under the power of God and will lie unable to move for ten or twelve hours."

Prophetic Utterance

The last days are upon us. The Master declared, "Occupy until I come." So continue to work. Continue to build His Kingdom. Continue to train men and women and boys and girls to go forth with the message of truth, the message of power, the message of the supernatural, and the message of the miraculous.

The enemy, Satan, knowing the time is short, moves in this day in his sphere and in his realm to work as never before. But at the same time, the Lord, in His realm and in His sphere, is moving to counteract the powers of darkness and to drive back the forces of evil. And so there shall come a greater manifestation of the power and the glory of God by the Holy Spirit.

If it were told to some what their role is to be in this move of God, they would not be able at the moment to accept it. But this move of God won't come all at once in a way that overwhelms people. It will come a little here and a little there and a little here and a little there. And when finally the Spirit of God moves with a mighty force, those who have a role in His plan will be prepared to obey what God has called them to do in the move of His Spirit.

And so, walk ye by faith. Walk ye in the light of the Word. And examine the Word daily to see if these things are so. And listen to what the Spirit says to your spirit. Yea, respond and be willing to follow the Spirit that resides in your spirit.

Be willing to let the Holy Spirit move and have His way in your services and in your church. Don't be afraid of fanaticism; don't be afraid of excess. Familiarize yourself with the Word and with the Holy Spirit. Encourage and invite the Holy Spirit to manifest Himself, and He will.

And the glory of the Lord shall rest upon His saints. Yea, the cloud of glory shall envelop many. And the eyes of many in the congregation will be open and they will see into the realm of the spirit. Many of those in the congregation will say, "I saw a cloud hanging over the minister's head as he preached." Others will say, "The preacher stood in that cloud as he ministered." And others will say, "I saw Jesus standing beside him!"

For this is the day of the miraculous. Man and miracles go hand in hand. Man and miracles are God's plan. The Father God has made the plan and set His power in motion.

So rise up, man! Claim your miracle! Rise up, woman! Claim your miracle! Yea, receive ye your miracle, for the miracle-working God is at hand.